**WILL POWER** is an award-winning playwright and performer. Plays include *Stagger Lee* (Dallas Theater Center), *Fetch Clay, Make Man* (New York Theatre Workshop, Marin Theatre Company, Round-house Theatre, True Colors), *Steel Hammer* with SITI Company (Humana Festival, Brooklyn Academy of Music), *The Seven* (Lucille Lortel Award Best Musical, New York Theatre Workshop, La Jolla Playhouse), *Five Fingers of Funk!* (Children's Theatre Company), *Honey Bo and The Goldmine* (La Jolla Playhouse) and two inter-nationally acclaimed solo shows—*The Gathering* and *Flow*. Power's numerous awards include a United States Artist Prudential Fellow-ship, and the TCG Peter Zeisler Memorial Award. Power's numerous film and television appearances include "The Colbert Report" (Comedy Central), and "Bill Moyers on Faith and Reason" (PBS).

Will Power was a guest of the U.S. State Department on five separate occasions, traveling to South Africa, Botswana, Lesotho, Turkmenistan, and Kyrgyzstan. On these trips and others, he taught community workshops in shantytowns, worked with poets in former regimes of the Soviet Union, and lectured at various libraries, gram-mar schools, and colleges. Power is currently on the faculty at The Meadows School of the Arts/SMU and the Andrew W. Mellon Foundation Playwright in Residence with the Dallas Theater Center.

# Fetch Clay, Make Man

# Fetch Clay, Make Man

A PLAY BY

## WILL POWER

OVERLOOK DUCKWORTH
New York • London

This edition first published in the United States and the United Kingdom
in 2016 by Overlook Duckworth, Peter Mayer Publishers, Inc.

NEW YORK
141 Wooster Street
New York, NY 10012
www.overlookpress.com
For bulk and special sales, please contact sales@overlookny.com,
or write us at above address.

LONDON
30 Calvin Street
London E1 6NW
info@duckworth-publishers.co.uk
www.ducknet.co.uk
For bulk and special sales, please contact sales@duckworth-publishers.co.uk,
or write us at the above address.

Cataloging-in-Publication Data is available from the Library of Congress
A catalogue record for this book is available from the British Library

Book design and type formatting by Bernard Schleifer
Manufactured in the United States of America
ISBN 978-1-4683-1109-9 (US)
ISBN 978-0-7156-5015-8 (UK)
1 3 5 7 9 10 8 6 4 2

*For my father, Chris, my mother, Gigi, and my wife, Marla*

# Preface

*Fetch Clay, Make Man* started as a photograph. I was back home
visiting family in San Francisco. On this day, I decided to stop by
Marcus Book Store on Fillmore Street. Here was a place that special-
ized in African and African-American books and periodicals. While
browsing on this day, I came across a fantastically large photo book
on Muhammad Ali. The book was elevated on top of a mantle, and
you had to use some muscle strength just to flip the pages, it was
that massive. The book contained some wonderful photos of the
champ, from early in his career all the way to present day. One of the
pictures caught my eye—Ali on the eve of his rematch with Sonny
Liston, he and his entourage looking defiantly at the camera, like they
were set to insert Ali and his legacy into the books of history. The
caption on the photo listed the names of the men who stood with Ali
during that critical time, when he had recently won the championship,
but was thought of as a fluke, sure to lose the rematch. He had also
recently come out as a member of the controversial Nation of Islam,
had befriended and then broken his friendship with Malcolm X, had
boldly changed his name and renounced Christianity, and in only a
couple of years would revolt against the massive entity that is the
U.S. Government in refusing to enter into the Vietnam War. Here was
Ali; young and pretty, bold, cocky, and ready to take on and overcome whatever the world would throw at him. And here were the men
who stood by him: his trainer, his bodyguards, his lovable sidekick
Bundini Brown, and with them just over Ali's right shoulder was
Stepin Fetchit. Stepin Fetchit? What?

    I learned about Stepin Fetchit as a child in the 1970s. I remem-
ber attending the pro-black, Malcolm X school for kindergarten. One
day Brother Kenyatta (a serious cat who wore his sunshades 24
hours a day, even inside when it was dark outside) was teaching us
about those who loved "The Man" more than they loved themselves.
He showed us a film about racial stereotypes, and the first person to
pop up on the screen was Stepin Fetchit, the old actor from the

1920s who made famous the stereotypical shuffling, lazy black man character. As I watched him, slowly moving across the screen, mumbling some indecipherable syllables to himself before falling asleep, I could see around the periphery of the room all of our teachers shaking their heads in shame. Before the scene was over, Brother Kenyatta couldn't contain himself, bursting out in a fit of anger. "You see this dude Stepin Fetchit? He is the ultimate sellout, young brothers and sisters! He is a traitor to our race! NEVER be like him!"

Growing up in San Francisco in the 1970s was a wild scene. Around me were the hippies, the protests, the drugs in the streets and in my home, and other psychedelic elements that one would associate with the city at that time. In the Fillmore district where I was raised, you had the extra layer of severe black militancy and the celebration and promotion of everything black. These were nationalistic times, and members of the community attempted to address the exposure that black Americans had to the lies of white supremacy by overcompensating-by believing that black culture was everything right, and white culture was wrong. So as a child I learned about Frederick Douglass and Harriet Tubman and the virtues of W.E.B. Du Bois, and when I learned about so-called white history I learned that Thomas Jefferson was only a slave master, and Andrew Jackson was only an Indian killer, and nothing more. These were serious times, when brothers wore afros and dashikis and black fists would be thrown into the air at the drop of a dime. I had cousins in both the Nation of Islam and the Oakland Black Panther Party across the Bay, my mother was a communist, and my father marched with King in Alabama as a member of SNCC. This was the world I grew up in. And within this world, there was no one more heroic, more a symbol of our manhood, than Muhammad Ali. He was everything we children wanted to be—bold, strong, intelligent, poetic, and he could whip anybody on the face of the earth. By this time, Ali had gone against the U.S. government and won, had beaten the seemingly unbeatable George Foreman in Africa, had defeated the awesome Joe Frazier in the Thrilla in Manila. Ali was so bad, D.C. Comics even made a special comic book called "Ali vs. Superman" in which Ali goes toe to toe with the Man of Steel. To us kids in the Fillmore, Muhammad Ali was Superman.

So you can imagine my shock when, many years later while browsing in a bookstore, I came across a photo of Muhammad Ali and Stepin Fetchit together. What's more, the caption listed Stepin Fetchit as Ali's friend and "Secret Strategist." What? How could this be? Staring at the photo, it was as if things I had learned from the past were being broken apart, an unquestionable truth being questioned. If these two seemingly opposite iconic figures were partners, what did that say about race politics and the complexities of American culture? This photo set me on a quest to discover if not the truth, then at the very least a better understanding of these two complicated, enigmatic figures and the world in which they lived. Once I began to explore this central relationship, I soon discovered others in Fetchit and Ali's world who were wrestling with their own issues of identity and image. All the characters in the play are trying to craft a public persona that suits them and supports what they wish to be. All the characters in the piece are masters of strategy, and like Ali, each one faces almost insurmountable odds in their quest to mold the mask.

*Fetch Clay, Make Man* took six and a half years to complete. I am forever thankful to Mara Isaacs, Emily Mann, Adam Immerwahr, and everyone at the McCarter Theater where the play was initially commissioned, developed and produced. I am forever grateful to Jim Nicola, Linda Chapman, and New York Theater Workshop for the continued development of this play, and for producing its New York premiere. I am incredibly thankful to the great Des McAnuff who directed the piece, and taught me things about writing and theater that I will utilize to the end of my days. And to the two amazing casts that were with us from the creation of the work through to its completion—John Earl Jelks, Sonequa Martin, Evan Parke, Richard Masur, Nikki M. James, Anthony Gaskins, Jeremy Tardy, Kenric Green, K. Todd Freeman, Ray Fisher, and Ben Vereen, to all of you thank you! And finally, to my agents—first Thomas Pearson at ICM, then Susan Weaving at WME, and to my family, my wife, Marla, and our children, Omar-Sol and Sophia, and to the entire community that raised me. Love and thanks to you all.

Will Power
May 2015

Fetch Clay, Make Man

The New York premiere of *Fetch Clay, Make Man* was
produced by New York Theatre Workshop
James C. Nicola, Artistic Director,
William Russo Managing Director


*Fetch Clay, Make Man* was originally commissioned and
produced by McCarter Theatre Center with support from
the NEA/TCG Residency Program for Playwrights.

# The Characters

**STEPIN FETCHIT**

**MUHAMMAD ALI**

**BROTHER RASHID**

**SONJI CLAY**

**WILLIAM FOX**

# Act I

## Scene 1

*Harsh lighting illuminates the stage, making the set appear as if it's part of an old black-and-white movie. Upstage there's a screen projecting stills of Stepin Fetchit in his various movie roles. After a few moments, enter* STEPIN FETCHIT. *He drags his feet and lazily shuffles along, moving downstage.*

### STEPIN FETCHIT

I don't know anybody'll mind if I stay over here and take a nap. I'm just so tired from sleepin . . .

I don't think the boss'll have to know . . . right here under this tree.

> FETCHIT *prepares for a nap. He then acts out seeing an angry plantation owner approaching him.*

Uh oh. Hello boss. No it ain't me, I'm out in the field, you know you just can't trust your eyes sometimes.

And uh I'm not me, I just look like me, but I'm somebody else.

Well if I see me, I'll tell 'im to get back to work.

> *The plantation owner is either convinced or frustrated. Either way he walks away.* FETCHIT *follows him with his eyes.*

I'll tell 'im, I'll tell 'im.

# Scene 2

*Lights up on* MUHAMMAD ALI *shadow boxing inside a small and hastily assembled dressing room.* BROTHER RASHID, *a small muscular man with a suit and bow tie, stands guard outside the door.*

*Projector screen: Lewiston, Maine, 1965*

STEPIN FETCHIT *reaches for a small matchbox suitcase and a flashy pork pie hat that covers up his bald spot. He then moves upstage into the set, approaching* BROTHER RASHID *at the door.*

BROTHER RASHID

I don't know why the champ wanna see you. You of all people.

*Calling from inside his dressing room.*

Brother Rashid!

BROTHER RASHID

Wait right here.

MUHAMMAD ALI

Say Brother Rashid!

BROTHER RASHID *leaves* STEPIN FETCHIT *in the hallway and enters* MUHAMMAD ALI*'s dressing room.*

MUHAMMAD ALI

Is he here?

BROTHER RASHID

Yes sir brother. The man just arrived on a bus from Boston. Shall I have one of the brothers show him to his room?

MUHAMMAD ALI

No, no I want to see 'im right now, send him in.

BROTHER RASHID

Of course brother, I'll send him in right now.

BROTHER RASHID *leaves the room and re-emerges in the hallway where* STEPIN FETCHIT *is waiting.*

Come right in, Stepin Fetchit.

BROTHER RASHID *steps aside and motions for* STEPIN FETCHIT
*to enter.* BROTHER RASHID *closes the door, standing guard
on the other side, leaving* STEPIN FETCHIT *and* MUHAMMAD ALI
*alone.*

MUHAMMAD ALI

Brother Rashid!

BROTHER RASHID *re-enters the room.*

BROTHER RASHID

Yes Brother Ali sir?

MUHAMMAD ALI

Is this Stepin Fetchit?

BROTHER RASHID

Yes brother it is.

MUHAMMAD ALI

Well what is he doin' in my dressing room?

BROTHER RASHID

Well I—

MUHAMMAD ALI

Why did you bring this coon to me man?

BROTHER RASHID

Well you said to send for 'im.

MUHAMMAD ALI

No I did not.

BROTHER RASHID

No, brother you told Herbert, and Herbert told me, and I sent word to
Chicago, yeah I did, had Brother Leon X search for 'im at the hospital.

MUHAMMAD ALI

Man, think Rashid, think why would I, the greatest of all times, I am the
greatest of all time ain't I?

BROTHER RASHID

Yes you are.

MUHAMMAD ALI

Am I not the greatest?

BROTHER RASHID

Yes brother sir you are.

MUHAMMAD ALI

So why would I, the greatest of all time, a champion to black people, want you to bring me this, this coon man, this Uncle Tom, this lazy, shiftless, man do you realize how much this chump has held our people back?

BROTHER RASHID

Yes, I'm well aware of that Brother Ali. I guess there must a' been some mistake, come on man, get out of here, leave the champ alone.

MUHAMMAD ALI

Oh no no no it's too late, it's too late for that see. 'Cause now I'm enraged. That's right I'm enraged and outraged by the sight of this darky, is he not the White Man's flunky?

BROTHER RASHID

That he is brother.

MUHAMMAD ALI

And how am I gonn' be the greatest of all time, if I let this traitor to our race just walk out of here. No no, it's time for payback brother. Close the door Rashid, and don't let nobody in here until I whip this sucker good.

BROTHER RASHID

You gonna—?

MUHAMMAD ALI

What did I say Brother Rashid? Close the door.

BROTHER RASHID

Yes sir Brother Ali sir.

*Exit* BROTHER RASHID.

MUHAMMAD ALI

Come on, come on Stepin Fetchit, put your dukes up, and take this beating like a man. Come on for once in your miserable wretched life, stand up and be a man!

> *With no alternative,* FETCHIT *removes his hat and puts his fists up, the look of pure terror visibly stained in his eyes.* ALI *lunges forward.*

MUHAMMAD ALI

Ahhhh!

STEPIN FETCHIT *flinches.*

STEPIN FETCHIT

Ahhh!

MUHAMMAD ALI

Gotcha!

MUHAMMAD ALI *laughs.* STEPIN FETCHIT, *realizing he's the butt of a joke, starts to laugh as well.*

STEPIN FETCHIT

You had me goin' there for a second Mr. Ali.

MUHAMMAD ALI

Man, you shoulda seen your face man, priceless. Say have a seat Mr. Fetchit, please make yourself comfortable.

*They sit.*

MUHAMMAD ALI

So uh, I wanted to meet you, and that's why I sent for you.

STEPIN FETCHIT

Well I'm here. So what ya want me for.

MUHAMMAD ALI

Well, I got this rematch commin' up in two days. Sonny Liston wanna take my head off, and I wanna keep my head on.

STEPIN FETCHIT

Well, it seems you breezed through the first fight you had with him. Why should you be scared of the second?

MUHAMMAD ALI

I never said I was scared. But I ain't no fool either, although the press would have you believe I am, you understand?

STEPIN FETCHIT

Yeah I do, believe me, I know all about that.

MUHAMMAD ALI

They sayin' I'm a fool,
And lightning won't strike the same place twice
But after this 'bout
We'll separate men from the mice

Now allow me to talk of mice and men
The challenger can't whup the champion

I'm gonna come so fast, like a piston
Straight to the dome of Mr. Sonny Liston

But wait Sonny's trained harder
Well this is what they say
He's gonna put a whuppin on you, you just wait Cassius Clay

But I'm the true champ
And Ali is my name

And even half my wits can't fit, into Sonny Liston's little brain

Because I am the boxer
With a mind that rhymes

I'm the prettiest, and the fastest
I'm the Greatest of all times!

But the truth is, Sonny is training harder see. Last time he did under-estimate me, and he won't do that again. This time he'll be prepared.

STEPIN FETCHIT

Well, can you whup 'im?

MUHAMMAD ALI

Of course I can. 'Cause while they're distracted with all a' that, I'm plannin' to come into the fight more equipped than I ever been before. And that's where you come in.

STEPIN FETCHIT

Me?

MUHAMMAD ALI

Yeah you. You knew Jack Johnson right?

STEPIN FETCHIT

Jack Johnson? Yeah, I knew Jack.

MUHAMMAD ALI

But I mean you knew him good, not casually or nothin', but real good.

STEPIN FETCHIT

We were friends, yeah. Now why you asking me about Jack Johnson?

MUHAMMAD ALI

Look here Mr. Fetchit.

STEPIN FETCHIT

Call me Step.


MUHAMMAD ALI

Alright Step. It's like this. They say Johnson was a talker. So he must of told you some things.


STEPIN FETCHIT

What things?


MUHAMMAD ALI

Well I don't know. Stuff that one old friend would say to another. See and I tried to find folks that knew Johnson well. But everybody he knowed like that, they all dead. 'Xcept you. The one and only Stepin Fetchit.


STEPIN FETCHIT

Mr. Ali, with all due respect, I don't know what you're talkin' about. Me and Jack had some good times, that's for sure. But he never told me nothin', and why would he? I'm a comedian. Besides, that was a long time ago, and my memory is . . .

> FETCHIT *makes a motion with his hands as if to say "so so."*

> *Pause.* MUHAMMAD ALI *goes to his locker and retrieves a small black-and-white photo.*


MUHAMMAD ALI

Look at this.


STEPIN FETCHIT

Where'd you get this?


MUHAMMAD ALI

One of the brothers got it for me. It says here it was taken before the Jeffries fight. I think they were signing the contract. Look Step, there must be like thirty white men all surrounding Jack—and some are against him, and some are his managers and lawyers, but they all white. And nobody's lookin' at him friendly.


STEPIN FETCHIT *(Looking at the picture.)*

No, not really.


MUHAMMAD ALI

But still, Jack went on to defend his title as the heavyweight champ of the world. But how did he do it? I wanna know how he did it. 'Cause he didn't have no bodyguards, no civil rights laws, just him.

STEPIN FETCHIT

Sure, but you ain't got to worry about that, 'cause it seems to me that you're well protected. No one can get you Ali.

MUHAMMAD ALI

Oh no? Well what about Kennedy, and he had the secret service, and still they couldn't protect him, they couldn't protect the President. So what chance does a black man have, especially one as pretty as me.

STEPIN FETCHIT

Mmmm, you get death threats don't you?

MUHAMMAD ALI

Everyday. They wanna kill me, they wanna get my family too.

STEPIN FETCHIT

They hate you. They hate your name.

MUHAMMAD ALI

I just want you to tell me what he said, that's all. So what you say?

STEPIN FETCHIT

Well, I guess I could tell you some stories he told me, and share whicha some of his philosopy on boxing. I don't think it's worth much, but uh . . . well what's in it for me?

MUHAMMAD ALI

Well, you can come to my sparring sessions, be ringside at the fight, you'll be part of the entourage for the whole weekend.

STEPIN FETCHIT

Are you gonna keep them Muslim goons off a' me?

MUHAMMAD ALI

Hey hey don't be commin' in here disrespectin' the brothers man.

STEPIN FETCHIT

No disrespect intended Mr. Ali. You know I'm a Catholic, and my kind and your kind ain't always seen eye to eye.

MUHAMMAD ALI

You a Catholic?

STEPIN FETCHIT

Plus everybody these days got it in they mind that I'm the White Man's boy, when nothin' is further from the truth.

MUHAMMAD ALI

Hey you can be my, let's call you my secret strategist, how's that? And you having a title and all, nobody up here is gonn' mess with you, 'cause you got a purpose now. So are you in?

STEPIN FETCHIT *thinks for a moment.*

I'm in.

*They shake.*

MUHAMMAD ALI

Well then Welcome Stepin Fetchit, welcome to my world.

STEPIN FETCHIT *and* MUHAMMAD ALI *shake on the agreement. Enter* BROTHER RASHID *in the hallway. He bangs frantically on the door.*

BROTHER RASHID

Brother Muhammad? Are you ok brother?

MUHAMMAD ALI *quietly tiptoes to the door and locks it, unbeknownst to* BROTHER RASHID.

MUHAMMAD ALI

Rashid . . . he's dead, Stepin Fetchit is dead.

BROTHER RASHID

He's d–? Well, look don't worry brother, I'll call Herbert, and we'll figure out some kinda way to dispose of the body. And then, and then we gotta get you out of here brother.

MUHAMMAD ALI

But I killed 'im Rashid. I meant to just beat him good, to teach him a lesson. But now he's dead.

BROTHER RASHID

Well brother you know what I say? I say good riddance. I never liked his movies anyway. Uh, are you ok brother? Can I come in?

MUHAMMAD ALI

Yeah come on—wait, wait he's getting up.

BROTHER RASHID

What?

MUHAMMAD ALI

He's getting—he was dead, I killed him, I just know I killed him. But now he's getting up, he's rising up.

BROTHER RASHID

Oh God, oh Allah no please not the champ, we can't lose the champ—
the door, it's locked brother!

MUHAMMAD ALI

Oh! He's got me around the neck. *This jigaboo's got me!*

BROTHER RASHID

I'm commin' Brother Ali sir, just hold on, I'm commin'.

MUHAMMAD ALI

Oh! It's the ghost of Stepin Fetchit, he's got hold of me!

BROTHER RASHID

Here I come Brother Ali I'm comin' man!

> BROTHER RASHID *opens door, at which point* STEPIN FETCHIT
> *and* ALI *laugh hysterically.*

MUHAMMAD ALI

I gotcha Brother Rashid, I got 'em didn't I?

STEPIN FETCHIT

Yes you did.

BROTHER RASHID

Um that's very funny sir. Well I guess it's silly, but I thought . . . I thought
somethin' was happenin' to you.

MUHAMMAD ALI

Naw I'm ok brother me and Step just talkin'.

BROTHER RASHID

Yeah well. Is there anything you need brother? Can I get you anything?

MUHAMMAD ALI

Naw naw, just show ole' Step here to his room, and see to it that he
gets back here early tomorrow mornin'.

BROTHER RASHID

Sir you gotta run scheduled for tomorrow.

MUHAMMAD ALI

Well bring him here after the run. Whatcha say Step, 6:30? 7 o'clock?

STEPIN FETCHIT

Sure.

MUHAMMAD ALI

Ok, bring him here at 6:30 am.

BROTHER RASHID

Ok brother.

MUHAMMAD ALI

I should be finished by then.

BROTHER RASHID

Let's go man.

RASHID *and* STEPIN FETCHIT *begin exit.*

STEPIN FETCHIT

Hey thanks for having me here Mr. Ali. I, I've been kinda blue for a while and, bein' in this new place with you, well I—

MUHAMMAD ALI

Man come on you ain't gotta thank me, just be here in the mornin' ready to tell me everything.


# Scene 3

*Lights up on* STEPIN FETCHET *and* WILLIAM FOX, *a 50-year-old pork bellied man with a cashmere sweater and a stiff arm.*

*Projector screen: Fox Studios, Hollywood, California, 1929*

WILLIAM FOX

. . . Now I saw you in several pictures you made for Louis B. Mayer, that shmuck. The last one—*In Old Kentucky*—you did a great job there Step.

STEPIN FETCHIT

Thank you sir.

WILLIAM FOX

Your sense of timing is amazing, and your use of pantomime is just extraordinary.

STEPIN FETCHIT

Thank you.

WILLIAM FOX

And when I saw you, what you did there, and the way the people were reacting to what you did, well. I knew I just had to have you for myself. So, let me say to you good sir, welcome to Fox Films.

STEPIN FETCHIT

Thank you Mr. Fox.

WILLIAM FOX

Don't mention it. Now did your lawyer have a chance to—, well who is your lawyer, do you have a lawyer?

STEPIN FETCHIT

Oh sure I work with Mr. Goldman, Mr. Goldman on Beverly Blvd.

WILLIAM FOX

Mr. Goldman on Beverly Blvd. Step I can't say I know him, and I know everybody in this town. Is this fellah new?

STEPIN FETCHIT

Yes sir, just blew in from Chicago.

WILLIAM FOX

And he works only with negro performers?

STEPIN FETCHIT

Negro and white sir.

WILLIAM FOX

Negro *and* white?

STEPIN FETCHIT

Yes sir. We can call him if you want.

WILLIAM FOX

No, no that's not necessary. So look here Fetch, did Mr. Goldman advise you on our offer?

STEPIN FETCHIT

Oh yes sir, and I have the contract right here, with Mr. Goldman's suggestions. Let's see. Oh, should we maybe call your lawyer in?

WILLIAM FOX

For what? I look over and personally see to everything here at Fox studios.

STEPIN FETCHIT

You don't have a—

WILLIAM FOX

Of course I got a lawyer, I got tons of lawyers, but it all goes through me. So, is that a signed contract?

STEPIN FETCHIT

Well not quite uh, like I said I have a few suggested changes from Mr. Goldman.

WILLIAM FOX

Changes? How many changes

STEPIN FETCHIT

14.

WILLIAM FOX

14?

STEPIN FETCHIT

In the first section.

WILLIAM FOX

In the first section? Are you crazy? That's a standard contract we give to all our new actors. And because I love your act and love the Fetchit character, I made sure to start you at five hundred and fifty dollars a week. Did you hear me? Not one hundred, not two, not three, not four, five hundred and fifty dollars a week. With the swipe of a pen you'll instantly become the highest paid negro in Hollywood. Do it now before I change my mind.

STEPIN FETCHIT

Mr. Fox I agree with you. In fact I thought five hundred and fifty dollars was too high to start with.

WILLIAM FOX

Don't bullshit me Step.

STEPIN FETCHIT

No bullshit sir. It's not good starting at such a high salary rate. I mean, down on Central Avenue, all the other negro performers are going to think I think I'm better than them.

WILLIAM FOX

What are you saying to me son?

STEPIN FETCHIT

Sir, I'm saying I agree with you that five hundred fifty dollars a week is more than enough, but Mr. Goldman thinks otherwise.

WILLIAM FOX

Well let's get Mr. Goldman on the phone, right now.

STEPIN FETCHIT

Sir, I'm sure you and me, two intelligent people, can keep the lawyers out of the meeting and work this out.

WILLIAM FOX

I hate lawyers. You know what I call 'em? Reptiles, that's right, they're all reptiles, slithering around in your pockets, stealing is what they do, taking from decent, honest, law abiding citizens like me. I work hard to be where I am. Every dollar I've made, I've earned it.

Yet no matter how much money you make, they always look at you like they're better than you, like they know something you don't. Even now, me, William Fox, the founder and top boss of Fox Films, but do they care? No, they just stand there, leaning on the bar at the Metropolitan Club, clustered together in a closed circle, laughing. Well, what else is there to do when everything's been handed to you on a silver tray?

Alright Stepin' Fetchit (FOX *glances quickly at his watch.*), let's go through the contract, and let's talk about the sections that your dear old Mr. Goldman is opposed to.

## Scene 4

*Morning. The lights come up on* MUHAMMAD ALI *and* STEPIN FETCHIT *in the dressing room.* RASHID *stands guard outside the door.*

STEPIN FETCHIT

As I back up, I can see more clearly what surrounds me. I'm crowding you like this up close, I can't see what's on the side or behind. But if I step back—

MUHAMMAD ALI

Yeah I know, that's how I fight. I'm stepin' back, but I'm gettin' you with this.

*ALI throws a few lightning quick jabs.*

STEPIN FETCHIT

Right now here's the thing. I'm still doin' what I want ya understand? I'm lovin' my life, partyin' and havin' a ball 'cause I'm steppin' back, and seein' everything and everyone around me.

MUHAMMAD ALI

Jack Johnson was a bad man.

STEPIN FETCHIT

Indeed he was. Alright here's somethin' else, here's somethin' Jack told me he would do. I want you to act out beatin' Sonny Liston. Pretend like it's tomorrow, and yall in the ring battling for the championship right now.

MUHAMMAD ALI

Aw yeah I do this all the time. Ok you ready?

STEPIN FETCHIT

I'm ready.

> ALI *begins to stick and move, circling a bench while jabbing with his left.*

MUHAMMAD ALI

Come on Sonny Liston, you big ugly bear, show me what ya got. That's it? That's all? Oh too bad for you Sonny, too bad for you. Huh? What? Oh no I'm not commin' that way, that was the last fight—that was Miami, we in Maine now. Can't come like Miami in Maine. But the truth is, you don't know how I'm gonn' come. But I'm dancin', gonna keep dancin' (*He throws a fast flurry of jabs.*), hah hah hah. There's the eye, I got your eye, now you see what I'm doin', you know my strategy, but it's too late-hah (*A jab.*), you're too far gone-hah-hah (*Two jabs.*), your goin' down-boom! That's how I see it.

STEPIN FETCHIT

Ok good, fine. Now, show me what's gonn' be like when you lose.

MUHAMMAD ALI

But I'm not gonna lose.

STEPIN FETCHIT

Still you should see it. You wanna talk about Johnson? Jack was a master of detail, in his mind and in the ring. Nothin' got past him, including how it would look if he lost. Said it made him stronger. Say if he saw all scenarios he could rule 'em all, and then pick which one he wanted. So now, show me you losin'. I wanna see Liston knockin' you out.

MUHAMMAD ALI

Step, come on.

STEPIN FETCHIT

What's the matter Ali you scared?

MUHAMMAD ALI

Heck no I ain't scared.

STEPIN FETCHIT

Ok, so let me see it right now, let's go.

MUHAMMAD ALI

Hah hah hah hah. I'm dancin', but Liston, he's trained harder this time.

STEPIN FETCHIT

That's right.

MUHAMMAD ALI

I'm movin'—hah, but he ain't tired like before, hah hah he ain't breathin' hard like before.

STEPIN FETCHIT

There ya go.

MUHAMMAD ALI

He ain't hittin' me but he's startin' to cut off the ring on me.

STEPIN FETCHIT

That's right.

MUHAMMAD ALI

Now he connects with a hook, and follows that up with two jabs. I'm stunned for a moment, but I'm not out, I'm still dancin'.

STEPIN FETCHIT

There ya go.

MUHAMMAD ALI

I get 'im with a couple a lefts, he brushes 'em off and keeps commin'. He ain't slowin' down this time, I try and move away, he gets in with three shots to the body—wooh, wooh, wooh, my kidneys shake, I spit blood, but I'm still dancin'!

STEPIN FETCHIT

Go ahead!

MUHAMMAD ALI

Now he gets me to the ropes. I'm in trouble, the champ is in trouble. Liston goes now to the head, jab, jab, now hook, jab—another hook. And now here it comes, the knockout punch, Sonny pulls back, then lets it go, a clean shot to my temple. My neck snaps all the way back, my legs let go, I fall, Clay falls, the Louisville Lip falls, the loud mouth nigger falls, justice prevails, America is saved, order is restored!

I don't see the point a' that. I'm gonna win, so why play out losin'?

STEPIN FETCHIT

'Cause if you see it, then you know it, then you rule over it. Now that's the makin' of a champion who lasts long.

MUHAMMAD ALI

I guess so. But that second scenario ain't gonn' happen. 'Cause I'm gonna whup Sonny so bad, that no one will ever second guess me again.

STEPIN FETCHIT

Say Ali, you gotta press conference later today right?

MUHAMMAD ALI

Yeah.

STEPIN FETCHIT

Well you think you maybe could say somethin' for me?

MUHAMMAD ALI

What you mean?

STEPIN FETCHIT

Well, you gonn' have the world listenin' this afternoon, and if you could tell 'em about me, about who I really am.

MUHAMMAD ALI

The press conference is about the fight.

STEPIN FETCHIT

Well ain't I part a' this fight?

MUHAMMAD ALI

I guess so.

STEPIN FETCHIT

You guess so?

MUHAMMAD ALI

Step, I don't mind talkin' to ya it's been fun, but if I tell the world you up here, well what are people gonn' think if they know I'm with you? That's not who I am Step, I'm the black man's hero, and you—

STEPIN FETCHIT

So you gonn' call me up here to tell you about Johnson, yet you too embarrassed a' me to even—

MUHAMMAD ALI

Step—

STEPIN FETCHIT

Look I'm not askin' to be at the press conference. Just say somethin' for me, that I am more than what they seen in the movies, tell 'im for me Ali.

*Pause,* ALI *is silent.*

Let's move on.

*Enter* SONJI CLAY *on the other side of the dressing room's door. She wears traditional Islamic clothing that covers her from head to toe. The only part of her body that's not covered is her face.*

BROTHER RASHID

Good mornin' sister Sonji.

SONJI CLAY

Hello Rashid. Is my husband in there?

BROTHER RASHID

Uh yes sister he is. Got a visitor though. Don't know if he wants to be
bothered right now.

SONJI CLAY

Well could you ask him?

BROTHER RASHID

Sure uh . . . is there something I can help you with? Maybe you'd like
me to relay the message to him when he's done with his session?

SONJI CLAY

No, no I'd rather see him myself.

BROTHER RASHID

Ok uh, wait right here.

> BROTHER RASHID *turns from* SONJI *and enters the dressing
> room.*

BROTHER RASHID

Uh excuse me Brother Muhammad, so sorry to bother you all but
sister Sonji would like to have a word with you.

MUHAMMAD ALI

Of course, send her in.

STEPIN FETCHIT

You want me to leave man?

MUHAMMAD ALI

Naw naw it's my wife, you should meet her anyway.

SONJI CLAY

Hey baby.

MUHAMMAD ALI

Hey hey baby.

> MUHAMMAD ALI *gives* SONJI *a polite, cordial kiss on the
> cheek.* SONJI *then grabs his head and thrusts it towards
> her face. They engage in a long, passionate kiss.*

MUHAMMAD ALI

Hmmm so sweet.

SONJI CLAY

Sweetest thing you ever tasted.

MUHAMMAD ALI

You the sweetest thing I'm ever gonna taste, hmm. Oh I'm sorry uh, Sonji this here is Stepin Fetchit. Step, this is my wife Sonji.

SONJI CLAY

It's nice to meet you.

STEPIN FETCHIT

The pleasure's all mine ma'am.

SONJI CLAY

You're Stepin Fetchit, the movie actor?

STEPIN FETCHIT

That would be me.

SONJI CLAY

Wow, I can't believe I'm meeting you. You know my father was a big fan.

STEPIN FETCHIT

Is that right?

SONJI CLAY

Yeah.

MUHAMMAD ALI

Your father liked his movies?

SONJI CLAY

He did. And he would always talk about 'em. How you made him laugh his head off when you would act lazy, you know so you didn't have to do the white man's dirty work.

STEPIN FETCHIT

But still get paid for it.

SONJI CLAY

Right. And all the way through the depression you kept my daddy laughin'.

STEPIN FETCHIT

Well I really appreciate that. Say is your father around? I would love to thank him for his support.

SONJI CLAY

No he's gone.

STEPIN FETCHIT

Oh, sorry to hear that.

SONJI CLAY

Yeah well, anyway it's nice to meet you.

STEPIN FETCHIT

You too ma'am.

SONJI CLAY

I won't take up too much of your time I just, I want to make sure you're coming home for breakfast?

MUHAMMAD ALI

Yeah, course I am.

SONJI CLAY

And I want to make sure they walk you all the way back, I don't want you to walk alone.

MUHAMMAD ALI

Of course they will.

SONJI CLAY

You're gonna come right back? You promise?

MUHAMMAD ALI

Do I—? Baby my main problem is how to keep you out my mind when I'm trainin'.

SONJI CLAY

You can't keep me outta your mind?

MUHAMMAD ALI

How can I? This mornin' I was joggin', tryna' focus on the fight, and all I could think about was Sonji, Sonji—Sonji.

SONJI CLAY

Really?

MUHAMMAD ALI

Yes really.

SONJI CLAY

You promise?

MUHAMMAD ALI

I promise.

SONJI CLAY

Then prove it.

> *They engage in another passionate kiss. After a few seconds,*
> ALI *breaks them apart.*

MUHAMMAD ALI

Uh, yeah, honey I gotta get back to what we was—

SONJI CLAY

Oh yeah yeah I know. I'm sorry, I'm sorry Mr. Fetchit. I just wanted to
make sure—

MUHAMMAD ALI

Baby, I'm protected. And after this I'm all yours, just me and you.

SONJI CLAY

Ok honey. (*Pause.*) Well, asalamalakum.

MUHAMMAD ALI

Walakum-asalam.

SONJI CLAY

Bye Mr. Fetchit.

STEPIN FETCHIT

Bye Sonji.

> *Exit* SONJI CLAY.

That sure is a fine lady you got there Ali.

MUHAMMAD ALI

Don't I know it. She got to be the prettiest negro woman in America.

STEPIN FETCHIT

I wouldn't doubt it. How long y'all been married?

MUHAMMAD ALI

Not long. But God knows from the moment I saw her, I was head over heels for that lady. I thank Allah everyday, 'cause he brought me Sonji.

*Enter* RASHID.

BROTHER RASHID

Brother Ali, can I get you anything brother? Somethin' to drink or somethin'?

MUHAMMAD ALI

Uh no I'm ok right now Rashid.

STEPIN FETCHIT

I'll take somethin' to drink. Can you get somebody to get me something to drink?

BROTHER RASHID (*Hesitates. Annoyed.*)

Sure. What would you like Brother Fetchit?

STEPIN FETCHIT

Y'all got any near beer?

BROTHER RASHID

We don't drink alcohol.

STEPIN FETCHIT

And I ain't askin' for alcohol, I said near beer. Near beer don't constitute alcohol, Ali do that constitute alcohol?

MUHAMMAD ALI

Uh I don't think so uh, go 'head Brother Rashid, send somebody to get some near beer for the brother, and I'll take an orange juice.

BROTHER RASHID

One orange juice for the champ, and one near beer for Brother Fetchit. Be right back.

*Exit* BROTHER RASHID.

STEPIN FETCHIT

What's with him man?

MUHAMMAD ALI

What you mean?

STEPIN FETCHIT

He ain't liked me since the moment I got here.


MUHAMMAD ALI

Aw don't pay him no mind, he ain't as dangerous as he looks.


STEPIN FETCHIT

He ain't?


MUHAMMAD ALI

Well, I mean he did his share of dirt, but that was a long time ago, before he joined the Nation.

Look, he's just trying to protect us.


STEPIN FETCHIT

Yeah, 'cause I heard your brothers talkin' 'bout Malcolm X. I know he just got killed, but still he got his followers. And they got lots a' guns.


MUHAMMAD ALI

So? Why should I care?


STEPIN FETCHIT

Isn't that why the fight got moved to Maine? I bet there's not a major city in America that would host this fight. Folks will watch it on TV. 'cause everybody worried about Malcolm's people. Are you worried about that?


MUHAMMAD ALI

'Bout what?


STEPIN FETCHIT

'Bout what everybody's been sayin'. That Malcolm's people wanna' take you out *for* what the black Muslims—


MUHAMMAD ALI

Shut up right now man. Don't you even spread no lies like what you 'bout to say.


STEPIN FETCHIT

What? I'm just tellin' you how folks is talkin'.


MUHAMMAD ALI

What folks? What folks is talkin' like that? The Nation had nothin' to do with Malcolm's death. We're a peaceful God fearing people, and we wouldn't kill another black man. We wouldn't do that to him. It's just not in our nature.

*Enter* BROTHER RASHID.

STEPIN FETCHIT

Brother Muhammad sir, the orange juice and the near beer are on the way.

MUHAMMAD ALI

Thank you Brother Rashid.

*Exit* BROTHER RASHID.

MUHAMMAD ALI

No more Malcolm talk man.

STEPIN FETCHIT

Forget I even brought it up.

MUHAMMAD ALI

I will. (*Pause.*) Ay Step, you excited about the fight?

STEPIN FETCHIT

Like you wouldn't believe Ali. I already picked out the outfit I'm gonn' wear.

MUHAMMAD ALI

What chu gonna wear?

STEPIN FETCHIT

Aw it's this really spiffy coat.

MUHAMMAD ALI

What color?

STEPIN FETCHIT

Blue, a nice blue coat, with off white pants that are so cleeeannn. I'm gonna look so good come fight night—wuu!—I might outdo my young self when I was—hey!—Headlinin' the Orpheum.

MUHAMMAD ALI

The Orpheum huh? Was that a cool place?

STEPIN FETCHIT

Aw it was the top of the line, a real classy joint you know? And I used

to come in like this and . . . well, you wanna hear me do my openin'
song?

MUHAMMAD ALI

Heck yeah, go 'head Step let me hear it.

STEPIN FETCHIT

Ok ok, listen . . .

> STEPIN FETCHIT *begins to sing and effortlessly glide around
> the dressing room.*

STEPIN FETCHIT

Richard
Can't get him up
Richard
Can't get him up
Richard
Can't get him up
Lazy Richard can't get him up

I was layin' down dreamin' Everybody was tryna wake me up

Like they was

Knockin
Rockin'
And re-boppin'

But see here I'm so sho'
I ain't gonn' open that door!

Richard
Can't get him up
Richard
Can't get him up
Richard
Just can't get him up
Lazy Richard can't get
Him
Up!

MUHAMMAD ALI

That was great man.

STEPIN FETCHIT

I aims to please.

MUHAMMAD ALI

So you still do shows like that now?

STEPIN FETCHIT

Uh, yeah when I can. No place like the Orpheum though, naw them days are long gone. But I'm all right, in fact, I've never felt better.

MUHAMMAD ALI

Yeah me too man, hey I'm in my prime, and you in your renaissance. Say Step, I need to ask you somethin', and tell me the truth now. Did Johnson ever say . . . well this is gonna sound crazy but, well I heard he had some kind of punch, it was called the Anchor Punch. And it was so fast, it could knock you out without the crowd even seein' it— whooooop!—just like that, and the other man was on the ground. And with his Anchor Punch, Jack could knockout not only the man in the ring, but any opponent, anywhere, whenever Johnson used it, all of his enemies would get knocked down.

STEPIN FETCHIT

Ali, I never heard a' nothin' like that. Whatcha call it? The Anchor Punch? Naw, Jack sure didn't teach nothin' like that to me.

MUHAMMAD ALI

Well I wish he did. Alright look here, I need to hit the shower, then I need to eat, I'm hungry man. Look, why don't we meet back here after I work out, let's say uh I don't know 2:30?

STEPIN FETCHIT

Uh sure ok.

MUHAMMAD ALI

'Cause you know we got that press conference at 3.

STEPIN FETCHIT

We?

MUHAMMAD ALI

Yeah we, we got a press conference I want you there with me. You ok with that?

STEPIN FETCHIT

Sure, sure press conference that'll be fine.

MUHAMMAD ALI

Things are lookin' good Stepin' Fetchit.

STEPIN FETCHIT

Yes indeed they are.

> *Exit* ALI. STEPIN FETCHIT *begins to cheerfully circle the bench, dancing and relishing the moment.*

## Scene 5

*Lights up on* WILLIAM FOX *and* STEPIN FETCHIT.

WILLIAM FOX

No no no, look I know your real name. But to the world you are Stepin Fetchit. Now and forever.

STEPIN FETCHIT

Please don't say that.

WILLIAM FOX

It's true. You're Stepin Fetchit. And when you talk like this in the *New York Times*, speaking of your fondness for concert recitals, Step you confuse the people, and then they hesitate with their money see. And we don't want that do we?

STEPIN FETCHIT

No we don't.

WILLIAM FOX

No we don't. We want the Fox audiences to be confident, assured, and happy they're going to the picture show to be with their old friend Stepin Fetchit. That puts money in the pockets, and that's what's important. So please stop complaining and do it, that'll be all Step.

> WILLIAM FOX *turns, as if to say "this conversation is over."*

STEPIN FETCHIT

Yeah, it's so easy for you to say Mr. Fox, you're white.

WILLIAM FOX

No, no that's where you're wrong Step. See I made a choice, I chose to be white.

STEPIN FETCHIT

What?

WILLIAM FOX

Oh come on, you're not the only slick one around here. You play a character, I play a character. My character is William Fox, the big man on top of the world here at Fox Movietone. And all this, the suits, my cigars, it's all an act. When we came here from Hungary, my family had nothing Step. And my father continued to have nothing until the day he died—nothing. And there we were, my mother and me, the oldest of 6 children, living in the worst dilapidated East Side tenement you can imagine. It was one of those places where the only water in the building was a shared pump downstairs. We lived on the 5th floor, you get me Step? I had to carry those buckets of water up that ricketty staircase day in and day out. One night I had two buckets, and I was rounding the bend that the stairway made from the 4th floor to the 5th, when I lost my balance and all the water came pouring out. I turned to go back down and fetch some more when it hit me, hard smack in the brain. This is my father's life, carrying water up five flights of stairs, spilling it, going back down to get more, carrying it up again, spilling it again, over and over. Do you understand what I'm saying to you? My father, he never advanced, never got ahead no matter how much hard work he did, he couldn't escape who he was.

Well, I decided right then and there on those muddy steps that I would play it different, play it cool, I'd become white. And it's the best thing that ever happened to me. Because now I have everything, everything! But do I miss being me sometimes? Sure. Would I trade the new me for the old me? Not on your life. Trust me, it's better on this side. And isn't that why you and I came to Hollywood in the first place? Huh? It's like we're all in one big movie out here, and as long as you play your part, we can all get rich. That's why I love this town. Where else can you make yourself into anything you want?

STEPIN FETCHIT

But I can't be anything I want out here, at least that's what you're tellin' me . . . Alright Mr. Fox. No more talking like that, "I'll talk like this" on and off the screen.

WILLIAM FOX

That's the spirit Step.

STEPIN FETCHIT

But I want a 30% increase in my weekly salary, and a chauffeured car paid for by the studio.

WILLIAM FOX

30%—? 30—that would make you one of the richest actors in Hollywood, more even than most of the white—

STEPIN FETCHIT

I'm not finished. In addition, since you've been leaning on me to be here on time.

WILLIAM FOX

Yes, especially if you're getting a 30%—you better be here on time.

STEPIN FETCHIT

And sir I plan to be. So I'm going to install a telephone in my house, just so you all can call me and wake me up every morning, but, I want Fox studios to pay for my telephone, the rental and the monthly bill.

WILLIAM FOX

Oh, this is preposterous.

STEPIN FETCHIT

And finally, I want a 14, no 24 karat gold hanger to drape my costume on.

WILLIAM FOX

Where the hell am I gonna find a 24 karat gold hanger?

STEPIN FETCHIT

And, I want my chauffeur, a white chauffeur no negroes, to carry my costume on the 24 karat gold hanger throughout Hollywood, keeping it pressed and cleaned.

WILLIAM FOX

Why on earth would you . . . Ok, alright look Step, these requests are highly unreasonable. Look let's call Mr. Goldman, maybe he can talk some sense into you.

STEPIN FETCHIT

Mr. Goldman?

WILLIAM FOX

Yes Mr. Goldman. I've never met the dodgy bastard but so what, come on, let's call him.

STEPIN FETCHIT

Mr. Fox, I guess you would've found out sooner or later. Well, I am Mr. Goldman.

WILLIAM FOX

You're—I don't follow you Step. See we need to—oh.

STEPIN FETCHIT

Mr. Fox, I really have to get into costume. Are we in agreement here?

WILLIAM FOX

Yeah, yeah sure, we're in agreement . . .


Scene 6

*Afternoon.* STEPIN FETCHIT *sits, sipping a can of near beer.*
*Enter* SONJI CLAY.

SONJI CLAY

Hello? Oh hey Mr. Fetchit.

STEPIN FETCHIT

Hi Sonji. And call me Step, please.

SONJI CLAY

Ok, Step. I didn't mean to—I mean, have you seen my husband?

STEPIN FETCHIT

Yeah, he went to shower off before the press conference.

SONJI CLAY

Oh he's in the shower?

STEPIN FETCHIT

Yep

SONJI CLAY

Uww. Let me take a peek.

SONJI *gestures to* STEPIN FETCHET *to be quiet.*

Shhh.

SONJI CLAY *quietly opens the door to the shower room*
*and stares at a naked* MUHAMMAD ALI. *She watches him for*
*several moments, admiring the muscles and curves of his*
*body. She then just as quietly closes the door.*

SONJI CLAY

He's so perfect.

STEPIN FETCHIT

Like a statue.

SONJI CLAY

And he's my man!

STEPIN FETCHIT

I know it girl. You caught yourself a good one.

SONJI CLAY

He got a good one too.

STEPIN FETCHIT

Yes he does. You're beautiful Sonji. Bet you done broke many hearts in your day.

SONJI CLAY

Well I don't wanna boast but . . .

STEPIN FETCHIT

Go on and boast girl. Say you want some near beer?

SONJI CLAY

Uh well, I'm not supposed to drink anymore.

STEPIN FETCHIT

Oh come on it ain't really alcohol, it's near beer. It's almost alcohol.

SONJI CLAY

Well I guess almost ain't the real thing right?

STEPIN FETCHIT

Right.

SONJI CLAY *takes the bottle and quickly takes a sip.*

SONJI CLAY

That's not bad.

STEPIN FETCHIT

I know. I used to drink this on the set all the time. I would tell 'em it helped me stay in character by making my eyes look all droopy. But really, I was tryin' to stay drunk so I could deal with they bullshit.

SONJI CLAY

Was it hard for you in Hollywood?

STEPIN FETCHIT

Honey you don't even wanna know. Hollywood was more racist than Georgia under the skin. A negro couldn't do nothin' straight, only comedy. So my plan was to break in with Stepin Fetchit, use him to become famous, but then add other characters, to show what I could really do.

SONJI CLAY

Well, sounds like you had a good plan. You give people what they want, then once you got 'em you can, you know let out who you are.

STEPIN FETCHIT

But it don't work that way honey it never does. Especially when you're good at the lie. When I tried to get out from under Stepin Fetchit's shadow, I couldn't. 'Cause when you wear the mask on for so long, you can't take it off.

SONJI CLAY

Are you bothered when people say things about you?

STEPIN FETCHIT

What things?

SONJI CLAY

You know, like you're a shufflin', no good—

STEPIN FETCHIT

Oh yeah ok those things. Yeah, it hurts. And see I'm tryin' to tell people that that's not who I am, I ain't the enemy. But I ain't about to pick up no gun, or put on no bow tie, that ain't me. I fight on the screen, that's my battlefield. And pretty soon, I'm gonna go back there and take back my title, as the greatest negro picture star that ever lived.

SONJI CLAY

How you gonna' do that?

STEPIN FETCHIT

Well, I'm thinkin', when people see me with your husband, they gonn' know I ain't no traitor. And when I go back to Hollywood, and it's knowed that I'm friends with the greatest, everything is gonna change.

SONJI CLAY

So you're usin' him?

STEPIN FETCHIT

I never said that.

SONJI CLAY

But you are. You're using my husband to resurrect your career.

STEPIN FETCHIT

Well ain't you doin' the same thing?

SONJI CLAY

Excuse me?

STEPIN FETCHIT

Oh come on honey. Look at you with that Muslim get up. I knowed from the first moment I met you that you wasn't at all about Elijah the messenger and all this nonsense. You a party girl right? I mean you like to party?

SONJI CLAY

You over steppin' your bounds Mr. Fetchit.

STEPIN FETCHIT

I know I am, that's what I do. Now answer my question, do you like to party?

SONJI CLAY

Ok look, I have converted to Islam, I am a Muslim woman.

STEPIN FETCHIT

Bullshit, you a foxy momma who loves the good life.

SONJI CLAY

I love my husband.

STEPIN FETCHIT

I never said you didn't. But Islam ain't for you, all this here, it's all an act, so don't be tryin to get all righteous with me and my intentions, if you gonna wear the mask wear it, but don't try and fool the fool, 'cause all you doin' is foolin' yourself.

    *Enter* RASHID.

BROTHER RASHID

Hey, what's goin' on in here?

                    STEPIN FETCHIT

What it look like man? Me and the lady talkin'.

                    BROTHER RASHID

You ok sister?

                    SONJI CLAY

Huh? Oh yeah, yeah I'm fine Rashid. I just came to look for Cassius.

                    BROTHER RASHID

Ali.

                    SONJI CLAY

What?

                    BROTHER RASHID

His name is Ali.

                    SONJI CLAY

Yeah I know. Well, I guess I'll meet you all at the press conference.

                    BROTHER RASHID

No no, Brother Ali wants you to meet him here so we can all enter together.

                    STEPIN FETCHIT

Wow, I ain't been part of a press conference in a long time.

                    BROTHER RASHID

And you ain't gonna be in one now either.

                    STEPIN FETCHIT

Come again?

                    BROTHER RASHID

You heard me. You ain't one of us, you far from being Muslim, so you shall have no place in a press conference about Muslims.

                    STEPIN FETCHIT

I thought the press conference was about the fight?

                    BROTHER RASHID

It is. But it's also about the Nation. And you ain't in the Nation.

                    STEPIN FETCHIT

I know that Rashid.

SONJI CLAY

Rashid stop gettin' all high and mighty, damn.


BROTHER RASHID

Sister—


SONJI CLAY

Yeah yeah sister sister, I know just relax man, ok? Now my husband wants Mr. Fetchit there, and if he wants him there he's gonna be there, you understand?


BROTHER RASHID *(Hesitates.)*

Yes ma'am.


SONJI CLAY

Now I'm gonna go back to the motel for a quick minute. Tell Muhammad I'll be right back, and then we can all go over to the conference. Ok?


BROTHER RASHID

Ok, I'll tell him.


SONJI CLAY

Thanks. Food for thought Mr. Fetchit, thank you.

> SONJI CLAY *kisses* STEPIN FETCHIT *on the cheek.*


STEPIN FETCHIT

Alright.

> *Exit* SONJI CLAY.


BROTHER RASHID

Man, are you crazy? Don't you ever kiss one of our sisters again.


STEPIN FETCHIT

Man she kissed me.

> BROTHER RASHID *moves towards* STEPIN FETCHIT *in a threatening manner.*


BROTHER RASHID

What you say?

> *Enter* MUHAMMAD ALI *from the shower room.*

MUHAMMAD ALI

This afternoon, we'll meet the press
And they still think of me as not being the best
But I am
A black super man
Without the S across my chest

Say Brother Rashid where's Sonji man?

BROTHER RASHID

She was just here. She say she'll be right back.

MUHAMMAD ALI

Alright well let's wait for her and then we gotta go. Say Stepin Fetchit
how ya feelin'?

STEPIN FETCHIT

I'm ok, uh. I'm thinkin' about sittin' this one out.

MUHAMMAD ALI

What the press conference? You don't wanna go?

STEPIN FETCHIT

Well, I'm kinda tired and uh.

MUHAMMAD ALI

Tired? What? Man I thought you lived for this kinda thing?

STEPIN FETCHIT

True but, well, uh I don't know.

MUHAMMAD ALI

Man I really want you to come, come on.

BROTHER RASHID

I think he's tired sir. You wanna rest Mr. Fetchit right? We can—

MUHAMMAD ALI

No Rashid, I want him wit' me.

BROTHER RASHID

But—

MUHAMMAD ALI

Rashid.

BROTHER RASHID

Ok Brother Ali sir, whatever you say sir.

MUHAMMAD ALI

Come on Stepin Fetchit, get ready to sock it to 'em man.

STEPIN FETCHIT

Ok but uh, well . . . uh what you want me to say when the press ask
what I'm doin' here?

MUHAMMAD ALI

Tell 'em whatever you want.

STEPIN FETCHIT

Really? I don't have to stick by no script or something?

MUHAMMAD ALI

A script?

STEPIN FETCHIT

Yeah like, is their something you want me to say, some kind of way you
want me to be when I speak to the cameras?

MUHAMMAD ALI

What? Heck no man, do whatever you want.

STEPIN FETCHIT

I can say anything I want?

MUHAMMAD ALI

Anything man. Heck that's what I do.

BROTHER RASHID (*Under his breath.*)

Yes we all know that.

MUHAMMAD ALI

What's that Rashid?

BROTHER RASHID

Nothing sir.

MUHAMMAD ALI

Naw it ain't nothin' man, I heard some sass in your voice just now.

BROTHER RASHID

Some sass?

MUHAMMAD ALI

Yeah some sass.

STEPIN FETCHIT

I heard it too.

RASHID *throws* STEPIN FETCHIT *a dirty look.*

#### BROTHER RASHID
Brother Muhammad sir I—, let me talk to you over here for a second brother.

#### MUHAMMAD ALI
No no no you can talk to me right here

#### BROTHER RASHID
No brother I think it's best if we—

> RASHID *puts his hand on* MUHAMMAD*'s arm as if to gently guide him to the other side of the room.* ALI *stays put and gives* RASHID *a look as if to say "what do you think you're doing?"* RASHID *drops his hand.*

#### BROTHER RASHID
Ok well . . . alright then here it is brother. There's some people a little upset about what you been sayin' or rather not sayin' at the press conferences.

#### MUHAMMAD ALI
What people?

#### BROTHER RASHID
People, some of the brothers that's over me.

#### MUHAMMAD ALI
Who you talkin' 'bout, what the Messenger?

#### BROTHER RASHID
No not the Messenger but—

#### MUHAMMAD ALI
Well then why should I care?

#### BROTHER RASHID
Because—. Ok I'm just supposed to relay a message to say that everyone in the Nation is very proud of you and what you been doin', but we'd like to hear you speak more about the teachings in the press conferences, that's all.

#### MUHAMMAD ALI
I'ma speak how I want Brother Rashid. You know me well enough to know that.

BROTHER RASHID

Brother just—

MUHAMMAD ALI

Look I talk about the messenger all the time You know this ain't last year or nothin' like that, I'm very up front about my faith and the truth about who is God.

BROTHER RASHID

I know you are. But still you confuse the people brother. You say you're for the liberation of the black man and woman, and yet you hire white people to train you to fight. Brother you can't allow this kind of thing to continue brother. It's weakinin' what we tryina do.

MUHAMMAD ALI

Rashid, Dundee, and Ferdie, they stay in the camp you understand? Look why are we talkin' about this, we already went over this man.

BROTHER RASHID

I know, and I'm not tryina' upset you brother, especially not before we meet the press. I'm just trying to show you that if you gonn' keep these white devils you got workin' for you all out in public for everyone to see, then at the very least you gotta put more Islamic knowledge into your public statements. I mean, isn't that what we're here for?

STEPIN FETCHIT

Hey Brother Rashid, I bet you ain't been part of no press conference.

BROTHER RASHID

I'm not talkin' to you Mr. Fetchit.

STEPIN FETCHIT

Well I'm talkin' to you. Now answer my question, have you ever been at the center of a press conference?

BROTHER RASHID

No I have not, what's the point?

STEPIN FETCHIT

The point is, you don't know what the hell you talkin' about. See 'cause if all Ali does is spew your Muslim rhetoric the press is just gonna take it, mix it up, and make you all look like bigger fools then you already are.

BROTHER RASHID

Brother Ali—

STEPIN FETCHIT

Ali's goin' about it in the right way as far as I'm concerned. You doin' it right man, you right to stay on your toes when you talk to the white press, you can't stick to no script.

BROTHER RASHID

Oh but you just asked the brother whether you should stick to a script.

STEPIN FETCHIT

That's 'cause I'm an actor. I know how to take a fabrication and make it look real, that's my specialty. But you? You too unskilled to do something like that.

BROTHER RASHID

Maybe I am but Ali ain't. All I'm sayin' Brother Ali sir is just to get more of our mission and our words up in the press conference that's all.

MUHAMMAD ALI

Alright Rashid, I'll try to get more in about Islam, just don't bother me with this no more.

BROTHER RASHID

Of course brother, I won't bring it up any more.

MUHAMMAD ALI

Are you ready Stepin Fetchit?

STEPIN FETCHIT

I'm ready Ali, let's dance.

MUHAMMAD ALI

How's my good side lookin'?

STEPIN FETCHIT

Lookin' good.

MUHAMMAD ALI

How's my bad side lookin'?

STEPIN FETCHIT

It look better than the good side.

MUHAMMAD ALI

'Cause I'm pretty.

STEPIN FETCHIT

That boy is pret-ty.

BROTHER RASHID *opens the door for* SONJI CLAY. *She has removed the traditional Muslim garb and now wears a short skirt with a blouse that shows off some cleavage. Without saying a word she quickly moves past* RASHID *into the dressing room.*

SONJI CLAY

Hey sugar.

MUHAMMAD ALI

Hey . . .

*They hug.* ALI *is confused by* SONJI*'s dress.* SONJI *pretends like she doesn't notice* ALI *and everyone's shock.*

MUHAMMAD ALI

Uh, can you all wait for me in the hallway, I'll be just a minute.

BROTHER RASHID

Of course brother.

STEPIN FETCHIT

Yeah no problem.

*Exit* BROTHER RASHID *and* STEPIN FETCHIT.

SONJI CLAY

How was the workout?

MUHAMMAD ALI

Good. I feel great.

SONJI CLAY

That's 'cause you are, you are the Greatest.

MUHAMMAD ALI

Who am I?

SONJI CLAY

The Greatest, in the ring and a few other places, you are The Greatest. (*They kiss.*) I love you Cassius Clay.

MUHAMMAD ALI

Love you too Sonji . . . Baby, what are you wearing?

SONJI CLAY

What?

MUHAMMAD ALI

Don't "what" me. Now I told you never to come out unless you have on the proper attire.

SONJI CLAY

This is proper for me.

MUHAMMAD ALI

You know what I mean. Now you gonn' go home and change into somethin' appropriate right now.

SONJI CLAY

I will do nothing of the sort. I'm dressed like any negro woman would dress—contemporary, sophisticated and a touch a' sass.

*Enter* STEPIN FETCHIT.

STEPIN FETCHIT

Uh excuse me, don't mean to disturb y'all, I just, I forgot my near beer.

FETCHIT *retrieves a can of near beer.*

Ok I'll wait for you all outside.

SONJI CLAY

Mr. Fetchit, what do you think about what I got on?

STEPIN FETCHIT

Honey I think what you have on is quite nice.

SONJI CLAY

See, there you go.

MUHAMMAD ALI

Look Sonji, it don't matter what Stepin Fetchit say. I'm your husband. And look you got all kinds of lipstick and eye shadow and everything, baby you don't need all that. See white women need that to look beautiful, but the black woman's beauty shines through all them products. Now go home and take all that off

SONJI CLAY

I said no.

MUHAMMAD ALI

Come on Sonji, please? Look Herbert and them gonna be here any minute, and so is the press, and I want you to look like a respectable Muslim woman.

SONJI CLAY

But I ain't no respectable Muslim woman.

MUHAMMAD ALI

Sonji!

SONJI CLAY

Mr. Fetchit can you excuse us for a minute?

STEPIN FETCHIT

Aw yeah sure, like I said I'll be outside with *Rashid*.

*Exit* STEPIN FETCHIT.

SONJI CLAY

Alright look chump, let's get one thing straight. When you fell for me, you fell for me this way, how I look how I am. And I never promised you anything else, I never said I was gonna' change me so you could feel more comfortable.

MUHAMMAD ALI

Yeah but you promised you'd be a Muslim, and follow the teachings of the Honorable Elijah Muhammad.

SONJI CLAY

But I didn't say nothin' about not being me. Now Cassius, you gotta back up a little bit or we gonna have some serious problems.

MUHAMMAD ALI

We already got serious problems. I'm the champ, and I'm tryna craft out a new image. Negro athletes don't have to be all ignorant, hangin' out with gangsters, doin' drugs and drinkin' alcohol. The champ of the world should be a clean cut, healthy, no drinkin' man, and that's what I'm tryina be, and—

SONJI CLAY

And you can't be that with me huh?

MUHAMMAD ALI

Sonji I love you baby, but, but that skirt is showin' way too much leg, that's all I'm sayin'. And Herbert thinks that—

SONJI CLAY

I don't care what Herbert thinks. Remember, I knew Herbert before you, and I've seen him at the nightclub I used to work at, and he would do some things that were way out of step with being a perfect Muslim, believe me.

MUHAMMAD ALI

You lyin' girl.

SONJI CLAY

Am I? Why you think he introduced us? He wanted your virgin butt to have a little kinky fun. It was all a joke to him, but he never thought we'd fall in love. Guess the laugh's on him now huh?

MUHAMMAD ALI

I don't like how you talk about the brothers Sonji. These are the men that protect me. And what will they say when the wife of the man they're protectin' keeps disrespectin' me and them by the way she dresses?

SONJI CLAY

So you're worried about what they think? Cassius, why do you care about them, they work for you. All that matters is how you feel. You need to run the show.

MUHAMMAD ALI

Why is that?

SONJI CLAY

Why is that? 'Cause you're the champ motha'fucka! Now stop actin' like a pussy and act like the champ!

>Pause.

MUHAMMAD ALI

Alright you can come and wear whatever you want. And I guess if the brothers say somethin'—

SONJI CLAY

The brothers wouldn't dare say anything, not to your face anyway. And if they start whisperin' behind your back so what, I mean what can any-body do about that anyway? (*Pause.*) Are you ready?

MUHAMMAD ALI

For what?

SONJI CLAY

For the press conference?

MUHAMMAD ALI

Oh, oh yeah of course. Let's get Brother Rashid and Step and let's go.

>SONJI *puts her arm around* ALI's *waist.*

SONJI CLAY

Yeah let's go baby.

ALI *and* SONJI *join* STEPIN FETCHIT *and* BROTHER RASHID *in the hallway. Scene shifts to the press conference.* MUHAMMAD ALI *takes center stage, flanked by* STEPIN FETCHIT *on the right and* BROTHER RASHID *on the left.* SONJI CLAY *is to the side and slightly behind the right shoulder of* STEPIN FETCHIT. *There should be an impression given that there are at least a dozen reporters surrounding them, as well as numerous TV cameras and flash photographers. We can't see these reporters, but we hear them as they begin to fire their questions at* ALI.

#### REPORTER ONE

Champ, what is your prediction for the fight?

#### REPORTER TWO

What round is he gonna fall in champ?

#### REPORTER THREE

Give us a poem about it.

#### REPORTER FIVE

Yeah you got a poem?

#### MUHAMMAD ALI

I cannot tell you the prediction, 'cause if I say what's gonna happen, and you tell the world, well they might not come.

#### REPORTER TWO

Why wouldn't they come champ?

#### REPORTER ONE

Yeah Cassius what ya got planned?

#### MUHAMMAD ALI

All I can tell you is that I'm working on some things, and believe me when I say, it will be a shocking, and dreadful night.

#### REPORTER FIVE

Sonny's the challenger, yet he's coming in a 9 to 5 favorite to win. Does that bother you?

#### MUHAMMAD ALI

All I can say is what I've already said. If you want to lose your money, bet on Sonny.

REPORTER ONE

What about the Muslims?

MUHAMMAD ALI

What about us Muslims?

REPORTER TWO

Is Malcolm X's followers coming to exact revenge?

REPORTER FOUR

Are you afraid?

MUHAMMAD ALI

I'm not afraid of nothin'. Allah is on my side. And soon the whole world will know the truth that Allah is with me.

BROTHER RASHID

Preach Ali.

MUHAMMAD ALI

And Allah cannot be beat, inside, or outside the ring.

REPORTER ONE

But what about Malcolm's people?

MUHAMMAD ALI

What people? Malcolm ain't got no people. Look, why don't you use your pens and cameras to turn attention onto these people that's commin' for me. If this is known to be true, then why is you and the police, and the FBI up here relaxin' with me? Why don't you go get them?

BROTHER RASHID

Tell 'em Ali sir!

REPORTER ONE

Alright well, tell us about your strategy for the fight.

REPORTER THREE

Yeah come on Clay.

REPORTER TWO

Yeah Clay, what's your plan?

MUHAMMAD ALI

How many times have I told you clowns, it's Muhammad Ali.

REPORTER TWO

Ok yeah whatever, but what are you gonna do?

MUHAMMAD ALI

Well first I'm gonna dance.

STEPIN FETCHIT

He's gonna dance.

BROTHER RASHID

That's right.

MUHAMMAD ALI

Second, I'm gonna dance.

STEPIN FETCHET

He's gonna dance.

BROTHER RASHID

Dance champ, dance.

MUHAMMAD ALI

And thirdly, you see this here. (*Ali holds out his right arm*).

PHOTOGRAPHER ONE

Oh wait hold that right there.

PHOTOGRAPHER TWO

Put your arm up a little bit.

MUHAMMAD ALI

Like this?

PHOTOGRAPHER TWO

Like that.

PHOTOGRAPHER ONE

Perfect!

PHOTOGRAPHER THREE

Now give us a mean stare, and open that mouth, bigger, bigger, yes there it is.

*Cameras flash wildly.*

REPORTER ONE

So you're gonna dance and hit 'im while you dance?

MUHAMMAD ALI

That's mostly what I'm gonna do. The rest I cannot reveal. But I will say this, which camera should—let me look into this one. I will say this. Sonny, if ya watchin', take this here as a warnin'. Get outta town now Sonny. I'm givin' you the chance right now to escape peacefully. I won't chase ya down, I won't come and get you if you just leave now! You make sure you get that to Sonny, ok?

REPORTER TWO

So what surprises you got in store champ?

MUHAMMAD ALI

Well I got the one and only Stepin Fetchit, the negro movie star of days gone by is with me, he's right here. You want him to say something?

REPORTER TWO

Well no, I just—

MUHAMMAD ALI

Say Step, come here man, the press wanna talk to you, now tell 'im what ya' feel.

STEPIN FETCHET

Uh, yeah hey everybody, I'm Stepin Fetchit.

REPORTER TWO

Champ, can we ask you, when you went against Sonny the first time—

MUHAMMAD ALI

Hey hey hey, Stepin Fetchit is standin' right here, the greatest actor in history, and yall ain't got nothin' to ask him about?

REPORTER ONE

Cassius we're sports writers.

STEPIN FETCHET

I can tell you a lot about sports, tell you about Satchel Paige and Jack Johnson. I knew 'em both, though I didn't get the chance to know Satchel too well see 'cause I—

REPORTER TWO

Champ, really, we wanna—

MUHAMMAD ALI

Hey hey the man is speakin', and yall need to listen. Go ahead Stepin Fetchit.

BROTHER RASHID

Preach on Stepin Fetchit.

REPORTER TWO

Champ, isn't this the guy that uh, the one from the old movies and all?

REPORTER FIVE

Yeah he's the one that used to do all that shufflin'.

REPORTER ONE

So champ, are you gonna shuffle in the ring?

REPORTER THREE

Yeah you gonna do the Stepin Fetchit champ? And turn lazy when ya fight, "uh yes sir boss abadubadubah!"

*The press laughs.*

STEPIN FETCHIT

I never said no abadubadubah, what the hell is that? You ask me some real questions.

REPORTER ONE

How does it feel to be an Uncle Tom?

REPORTER TWO

How does it feel to be hated by your own people?

STEPIN FETCHIT

My own people who?

REPORTER TWO

Negroes.

STEPIN FETCHIT

I'm not hated by all negroes, only some. And even those . . . they don't understand that's all.

REPORTER FIVE

What are you doin' here in Maine Stepin Fetchit?

STEPIN FETCHIT

I'm here with Ali. I'm his, I'm his secret strategist.

REPORTER TWO

His what?

REPORTER FIVE

So you're the mastermind behind the new champ? You? Stepin Fetchit? Christ now I've heard everything.

REPORTER TWO

Well what are you strategizing? You showin' Ali how to take a punch?

REPORTER ONE

How to fall and get back up.

REPORTER THREE

No no he's teachin' him how to lean against the ropes, lean all the way back and take a nap.

REPORTER TWO

Say that was prettty good there.

REPORTER ONE

He's a poet like you champ.

REPORTER TWO

How about a poem for the fight.

MUHAMMAD ALI

Stepin Fetchit ain't finished talkin'.

REPORTER ONE

But—

MUHAMMAD ALI

Let him finish havin' his say. Go 'head Stepin Fetchit, speak on man.

BROTHER RASHID

Speak on Brother Fetchit, speak on.

STEPIN FETCHIT

You see me on the screen, but you don't understand what I was doin'. Now you go back, and look at them films, go look at 'em, go see how

I made somethin' from nothin'. You wanna talk about Malcolm X? You wanna talk about Dr. King? I was the first negro militant (*The press laughs at the suggestion.*) No, no don't you . . . listen to me! I defied white supremacy.

BROTHER RASHID

Tell the truth brother.

STEPIN FETCHIT

There was no white man's idea a' making a negro picture star. I was the first of my race to receive a screen credit. In Hollywood we were seen but never heard, faces with no names. I fought hard to get us a name, and in doin' so proved that negroes were equal. And I made some sacrifices but . . . but let me say this right now. I'm more than Stepin Fetchit. My name is Lincoln. Lincoln Perry. And you wanna call me an Uncle Tom?

BROTHER RASHID

That's what they wanna do.

STEPIN FETCHIT

Well if I am, then that's a great compliment.

BROTHER RASHID

There it is, there it is.

STEPIN FETCHIT

'Cause Tom was a good man, and the world's first integrationist.

BROTHER RASHID

Tell the truth brother.

STEPIN FETCHIT

So go 'head call me an Uncle Tom, it don't do nothin' to me, it makes me proud. See now the one you talkin' about who really sold us out, that would be little black Sambo. With his eyes popped out, forever scared, forever a boy. Well I ain't no boy.

BROTHER RASHID

No sir!

STEPIN FETCHIT

And I ain't never.

BROTHER RASHID

He ain't never.

STEPIN FETCHIT

I say I ain't never.

BROTHER RASHID

He ain't never.

STEPIN FETCHIT

. . . been no Sambo.


END OF ACT I

# Act II

## Scene 1

*Bold, colorful lighting floods the stage. The projector screen projects oversized photos of Muhammad Ali in various defiant poses. Enter* MUHAMMAD ALI. *He confidently walks downstage center. The walk quickly breaks into a vigorous shadow boxing session.*

MUHAMMAD ALI

Back up
Back up sucker
You can't defeat me
'Cause I'm fast
And strong
And pretty as a girl
I can't possibly be beat

You don't believe me?

Well just today, I wrassled with a elephant
And tussled with a shark
In case there's ever a flood
I put two of me on Noah's Ark
And I can go without water
Like a camel on the sand
I went to the jungle in Africa
And beat the crap outta Tarzan
But I couldn't do nothin' for Jane
'Cause that ain't my thang
My lungs are so large
I blew out a hurricane

I'm the baddest black man
In the whole entire world . . .

Hey back up
Back up sucker!
All the way back where I can see
And once I get that Anchor Punch
No one will defeat me

*Projector screen: Lewiston, Maine. Day of fight.*

## Scene 2

*Lights up on* STEPIN FETCHIT *and* MUHAMMAD ALI, *laughing.* ALI *has just returned from his daily run. He wipes the excess sweat from his body as* FETCHIT *sits on a bench toying with his hat.*

MUHAMMAD ALI

Man we had 'em goin there didn't we? Didn't we?

STEPIN FETCHIT

Yeah we did. It felt good to be up there witcha. All them reporters and everything. I tell ya Ali, I had damn near forgot about, about what it is to be a star. One day maybe I'll be there again.

MUHAMMAD ALI

Maybe so, who knows. I mean you ain't lost none a' your actin' skills have you?

STEPIN FETCHIT

Heck no. I'm still just as sharp and keen as I ever was. I just need a break that's all. One break and I'm back on top. I'm the biggest star you have under contract, and I know you're not dumb enough to throw all this money away 'cause a some parking tickets.

*Enter* WILLIAM FOX.

WILLIAM FOX

It's not about parking tickets, it's about our image. And you have proven to go against that with your recklessness, which includes the driving tickets, the shouting matches, the tardiness . . .

STEPIN FETCHIT

Well maybe if I could play somethin' besides a fool on the screen, I wouldn't have to act like one off the screen.

WILLIAM FOX

Step, ya had the whole world by the balls *and* you let it go! From now on you have no place at the table. You're out of here, you're done, it's over!

*Exit* WILLIAM FOX.

STEPIN FETCHIT

Say Ali, you ever think about making a movie?

MUHAMMAD ALI

What kind of movie?

STEPIN FETCHIT

Well like a feature, about you, about your story. It would give you a chance to set the record straight. I mean all these reporters is only gonna write you the way they see you. But if you made a movie, then all your fans would get to know the real you, the real Ali. And, you could make a whole buncha money.

MUHAMMAD ALI

Yeah but what I need to make a movie for Step? I'm on TV 24 hours a day.

STEPIN FETCHIT

But they still controllin' it. But if you and I made a movie.

MUHAMMAD ALI

The Greatest . . .

STEPIN FETCHIT

It could be called The Greatest.

MUHAMMAD ALI

Well I guess I would look good on the big screen.

STEPIN FETCHIT

You would look great boy. Just think, all that prettiness you got, magnified twenty five times! So let's get a script together and start plannin' this thing out.

MUHAMMAD ALI

Well, there is a man in Chicago, a Muslim brother, James X. Now he's been known to dabble in film every now and then.

STEPIN FETCHIT

Yeah.

MUHAMMAD ALI

He the one that oversees all the filming for Saviours' Day. I bet if we ask him to direct the movie he would do it.

STEPIN FETCHIT

Yeah he probably would but, we need to make sure we get the best. Now John Ford, he's a good friend of mine and a first rate director. Can you imagine what he would do with your story? Look here, Muhammad Ali, and Lincoln Perry in The Greatest, directed by John Ford. Oh man I'm tellin' you, we'd have cinematic smash on our hands.

MUHAMMAD ALI

But ain't John Ford the guy that do all them Westerns?

STEPIN FETCHIT

That's him.

MUHAMMAD ALI

Well, I like a Western as much as the next guy, but I just can't see it for my story, no we got to get a brother in the Nation to do it. If you sayin' you concerned about how the White Man bends the way I look and what I say on television, well what's to say John Ford wouldn't do the same thing?

STEPIN FETCHIT

'Cause he's my friend.

MUHAMMAD ALI

But he ain't one a us, and no tellin' what he might do, damn he might have me gettin' beat up by some old cowboy or something. Now what would my fans say if they go to the movies and see me, the greatest of all times, gettin' beat up by some cowboy. I mean I wouldn't mind if I lost to the Mummy or something like that, 'cause they got supernatural powers. Plus the Mummy is from Eygpt, and Eygpt is in Africa, which means the Mummy is a brother you dig? And if I gotta get knocked out, I'd rather lose to a supernatural brother than a raggedy old cowboy. Man I could see it now, the new Black man vs. the old Black man. And then at the end, right as we about to get it on, we realize that despite our differences, we one in the same. Only thing is he wrapped up in all them bandages and you can still see me pretty, but besides that we both the same, two black men, and me and the Mummy join in the struggle together. Now that would be a movie.

STEPIN FETCHIT

Well, we could do that one, but maybe that's the second or third movie we do. You know 'cause once we film The Greatest, well that's gonna turn you into a movie star, they'll give you a contract and—

MUHAMMAD ALI

I don't want the White Man's contract Step.

STEPIN FETCHIT

But it'll be a good one, a fair one, and—

MUHAMMAD ALI

But I don't want all that. If I wanted to sign up with them, I woulda had a white manager instead a' Herbert, I woulda been with a white organization instead of the Muslims. No I'm not signin' no agreement with the likes of the White man.

*Enter* BROTHER RASHID.

BROTHER RASHID

Brother Muhammad, can I talk to you for a second *brother*, in private?

*Pause.*

STEPIN FETCHIT

Yeah whatever, I'll be in the hallway.

*Exit* STEPIN FETCHIT.

BROTHER RASHID

Brother Ali, what the hell was that?

MUHAMMAD ALI

That? That what?

BROTHER RASHID

At the press conference. Stepin Fetchit was up there talkin' crazy while the whole world listened, and you let him.

MUHAMMAD ALI

Well you was backin' him up too Brother Rashid. I heard you man.

BROTHER RASHID

Yeah 'cause I had no choice. We gotta show a united front. Even though I can't stand Stepin Fetchit, when in public I still got to back that clown up.

MUHAMMAD ALI

And I'm sure he appreciates that.

BROTHER RASHID

It was the hardest thing I've ever done in my life. I wanted to just strangle that coon.

MUHAMMAD ALI

You hate him that much Rashid?

BROTHER RASHID

With a passion sir. And I wish you would just send him on his way. I mean the fight's tonight, and I think you need to really focus now and stop all this foolishness that you've been doin'.

MUHAMMAD ALI

But Step's ok man, he ain't causin' nobody no real harm.

BROTHER RASHID

Oh no? Well wait 'till the Messenger hears about the press conference. I mean Uncle Tom was a great man? I tell you, me and you gonn' be in big trouble.

    *Enter* STEPIN FETCHIT.

STEPIN FETCHIT

Uh excuse me. Don't mean to disturb yall meeting but uh, if I'm not needed, I'd like to take a quick rest in the motel.

MUHAMMAD ALI

Sure no problem I'll send for you later. Say Rashid, can ya escort Mr. Fetchit back to his sleepin' quarters?

BROTHER RASHID

No. Mr. Fetchit can escort hisself over there.

MUHAMMAD ALI

Excuse me?

STEPIN FETCHIT

What, you too good to walk me, the Muslim's guest, back to my motel?

BROTHER RASHID

Ain't nobody gunnin' for you old man. I'm stayin' here with Brother Muhammad, we got things to talk about, real things. Now I'm sure you wouldn't mind walkin' yourself—

STEPIN FETCHIT

I do mind.

MUHAMMAD ALI

Yeah and I mind too. Rashid what's gotten into you man? Regardless of his politics or his past, he is our guest. Now do as I say and escort him back over—

#### BROTHER RASHID

I said no Brother Muhammad sir. We needs to finish talkin'. And what we need to talk about is a matter of great importance and personal safety. Plus a ton a' other things on my mind, none of which is the well-being of Mr. Fetchit.

#### STEPIN FETCHIT

But that's your job!

#### BROTHER RASHID

Nigger don't tell me my job, I know what I'm supposed to do.

#### MUHAMMAD ALI

Whoa Rashid, come on there's no need for that kind of language man.

#### BROTHER RASHID

What? You tryna' reprimand me brother? When this gorilla stands here in direct contradiction to everything we believe in, and he insults me, talks down to me, and you gonn' stand with him?

#### STEPIN FETCHIT

Ali, this guy is way out of line. I say you fire him, right now.

#### BROTHER RASHID

Say what?

#### STEPIN FETCHIT

You a servant chump, and you went against a direct command and—

#### BROTHER RASHID

What did you call me? A servant? Man, I will hurt you bad, done did it to men for far less.

#### MUHAMMAD ALI

Ok nobody's gonna hurt nobody. Rashid you stay with me, Mr. Fetchit you go on 'head back to the motel room.

#### STEPIN FETCHIT

What? You mean he ain't gonna escort me?

#### MUHAMMAD ALI

You want him to escort you? After this blow up? No, I don't advise that, look just go on Step. I'll send Rashid to get you in a little while, after we've all calmed down.

(Pause.)

Go ahead Step, I'll send for ya later.

STEPIN FETCHIT

Alright.

STEP *turns to leave.* ALI *looks at* RASHID *as if to say, "aren't you gonna say something?" Finally, after several moments.*

BROTHER RASHID

Asalamalakum.

STEPIN FETCHIT

Walakum-asalam.

*Exit* STEPIN FETCHIT.

MUHAMMAD ALI

What's wrong with you man?

BROTHER RASHID

What's wrong with me? After what he said to me, how you gonn' ask me that man?

MUHAMMAD ALI

Step was wrong, but you've been trained to keep cool. Now all that training goes down the drain, why?

BROTHER RASHID

I don't know. The old man gets under my skin that's all.

MUHAMMAD ALI

No that ain't all Brother Rashid. Now come clean man, and say what's on your mind.

Pause.

BROTHER RASHID

It's been confirmed. A carload of Malcolm's people are in fact commin' up here from New York.

MUHAMMAD ALI

How you know that?

BROTHER RASHID

We've been in communication with the FBI. They say a number of Malcolm's men have not been where they usually are, and the FBI says they're headed this way. They're gonna try to take you out brother.

MUHAMMAD ALI

We been talkin' to the FBI?

BROTHER RASHID

Yes sir, that's how we've been gatherin' some of this information. A necessary evil Herbert calls it. But . . . I mean they call themselves protecting us but I don't trust the FBI Brother Ali sir. And on top of that, Liston's here with his people, and who knows what they might do. Not to mention the local police, who I'm sure wouldn't mind taking a crack at you if they get the chance. And we are prepared, as much as we can be. But I don't know if it's gonn' be enough. 'Cause all it takes is one bullet. One bullet, shot from a gun held by one hand. That's all it takes. (*Pause.*) Are you ok Brother Ali sir?

MUHAMMAD ALI

Yeah I'm ok, I just wanna box man, that's all.

BROTHER RASHID

I understand.

MUHAMMAD ALI

And it's one thing to kill me, if Allah decides it's my time what can I do about that? But my mother will be there tonight, and my wife. What about them? What if a stray goes in their direction and hits them?

BROTHER RASHID

I know. And we're doing everything possible to—

MUHAMMAD ALI

Well make sure you do Rashid. I tell you if anything happens to my wife, I swear . . .

BROTHER RASHID

Brother, I'm sorry I involved you in all this. You don't need to be knowin' all a' what we are concerned about. Just try and focus on the match.

MUHAMMAD ALI

I'ma beat all them suckas if I have to, you understand Brother Rashid? I'ma whup all of 'em. 'Cause all mighty Allah is on my side!

BROTHER RASHID

This is true.

MUHAMMAD ALI

I only speak the truth Rashid. Now let's get to work, we got work to do brother, we got a championship to defend.

BROTHER RASHID

Yes sir Brother Ali sir.

MUHAMMAD ALI

And I got my workout in 20 minutes. So we got some time now, go catch Step for me and tell 'em to come on back

BROTHER RASHID

But, why?

MUHAMMAD ALI

Just go get 'im Rashid, I don't have much time man.

BROTHER RASHID

Uh yes sir, I'll bring him here right away Ali sir.

BROTHER RASHID *begins to exit.*

MUHAMMAD ALI

Brother Rashid?

BROTHER RASHID

Yes brother?

MUHAMMAD ALI

Why did Malcolm have to die?

BROTHER RASHID

Hey, I don't know nothin' about that brother. You know I've been with you this whole time. I don't know who did it, how they did it, or even if it was Muslims or not. But don't feel too bad for Brother Malcolm now, 'cause see, he got what he deserved.

MUHAMMAD ALI

How can you say that man?

BROTHER RASHID

It's the truth Brother Ali that's how I could say it. He went against the Messenger, and the punishment for that is death.

MUHAMMAD ALI

What? No, that's not—man you don't understand Brother Rashid. Malcolm was my friend.

BROTHER RASHID

Hey I loved Malcolm too brother, he taught me too. In fact, it was Malcolm that turned me towards Islam when I was still Canard Jenkins.

Shoot I had the conk and the gator shoes I was such a fool. But Malcolm, he still talked to me. He say it's time for you to protect your brothers and sisters. And put your people first for a change, instead a' always putting the white man first.

That day on the corner he talked and I listened, and it all started to make sense. And I was about to sign up right there on the spot, until he started preachin' about not eatin' no pork. I was like wait a minute now. No more robbin' my people, ok, no more lustin' after fast women, no problem. But no pork? Now you gettin' crazy now Brother Malcolm. But I came around, gave up everything to be in the Nation, and it was all 'cause a' Malcolm. So believe me when I say that I don't take none of this lightly.

But he is a traitor Brother Ali. He was askin' you and me and all a' the Nation to make a choice, man what kind of choice is that for us to make? Before Malcolm, before my love for you brother, first and foremost we are Muslims, and we follow the Honorable Elijah Muhammed, and he want us to leave him? What kind a' craziness is that? Is Elijah not the prophet, the messenger sent from Allah to free the black man? No, we must stand firm behind the Messenger, and stomp out anything that stands in the way.

MUHAMMAD ALI

But he didn't have to die.

BROTHER RASHID

I told ya I don't know nothin' 'bout that now. And neither do you, understand?

MUHAMMAD ALI

But I didn't do anything to help him. I coulda' done somethin', I shoulda' done somethin' to help him.

BROTHER RASHID

Don't talk like that around here Brother Ali sir. That kind a talk ain't healthy, if you know what I mean.

MUHAMMAD ALI

No I don't know what you mean Brother Rashid, please tell me what you mean?

BROTHER RASHID

Nothin' Ali just, hey now look brother, you are the champ, but you're also a young man, and you tryna' hold on to your championship, now that's what I want you to focus on, not Malcolm or nobody else, just the fight. 'Cause see if Liston knocks you out, that's gonna make you and everybody in The Nation look bad.

MUHAMMAD ALI

I'm not gonna get knocked out Brother Rashid. I'm the Greatest of All
Times.

BROTHER RASHID

That's right Brother Ali sir, you are the Greatest.
You float like a butterfly, and sting like a bee.

MUHAMMAD ALI

Your hands can't hit what your eyes can't see.

MUHAMMAD ALI AND BROTHER RASHID

Rumble young man rumble!

MUHAMMAD ALI

Right. Ok go get Stepin Fetchit.

BROTHER RASHID

Right away Brother Ali sir.

> *Exit* BROTHER RASHID. MUHAMMAD ALI *pauses for a moment.*
> *Enter* SONJI CLAY.

SONJI CLAY

Hey Sugar.

MUHAMMAD ALI

Sonji, what are you doin' here?

SONJI CLAY

What you don't want to see me?

MUHAMMAD ALI

Of course I do. I'm just tryna figure out how you slipped past—

SONJI CLAY

Who the brothers? Please, they're so predictable, I hope you don't
think they're protectin' you.

MUHAMMAD ALI

Well—

SONJI CLAY

I'm just playin' baby, your "brothers" are right outside.

MUHAMMAD ALI

Oh, oh yeah of course, of course.

SONJI CLAY

You're so gullible Cassius. Like the first time we went out.

MUHAMMAD ALI

And you told me you'd never been on a date before.

SONJI CLAY

Meanwhile, I'm sayin' hello to everyone in the club.

MUHAMMAD ALI

And I'm askin' you, how you know this person or that person.

SONJI CLAY

And then remember, when we got on the dance floor—

MUHAMMAD ALI

What were they playin'?

SONJI CLAY

Shotgun!

MUHAMMAD ALI

Yeah "shotgun."

SONJI CLAY

Yeah but wait you're off.

MUHAMMAD ALI

I'm off?

SONJI CLAY

Yeah Junior Walker sings it "shotgun."

MUHAMMAD ALI

Well, Muhammad Ali sings it "shotgun."

SONJI CLAY

Look baby, listen—
SHOTGUN.

SONJI CLAY AND MUHAMMAD ALI

SHOOT 'IM FOR HE RUNS NOW
DO THE JERK BABY
DO THE JERK, NOW
HEY . . .

> SONJI CLAY *and* MUHAMMAD ALI *make out. They begin to peel each other's clothes off.*

SONJI CLAY

Cassius I love you so much. More than anyone I've been with.

MUHAMMAD ALI

How many men have you been with? How many have you been with before me?

SONJI CLAY

What?

MUHAMMAD ALI

How many men—

SONJI CLAY

I don't know . . . what is it? What's wrong now?

MUHAMMAD ALI

What's wrong? I'll tell you what's wrong. A woman lyin' to her husband, that's a sin Sonji. 'Cause you told me, you say "I've been on some dates, and I used to work at this club," but you told me that you never been with a man. Now did you not tell me that?

SONJI CLAY

Yeah but, well I knew that's what you needed to hear. I was trying to comfort you.

MUHAMMAD ALI

I don't need you to comfort me, I was the champ of the world, what I need you to comfort me for?

SONJI CLAY

Because you were nervous. I could tell out there on the dance floor, I could tell just by the way you moved that you didn't know too much.

MUHAMMAD ALI

So you decided it was better to hide your past from me?

SONJI CLAY

No I just didn't think it necessary to tell you my whole life story on our first date.

MUHAMMAD ALI

But we not on our first date, we're married now. And you have yet to— when were you going to tell me this?

SONJI CLAY

It was none a' your business Cassius. My daddy and momma died when I was young, and I had to fend for myself and that's the way I did it, I had boyfriends and they took care of me—so what?

MUHAMMAD ALI

Aw Sonji, baby how could you not tell me that?

SONJI CLAY

Because you didn't wanna hear about it. No *man* does. Yeah now you say you wanted me to be me, but would you really have asked me out again if you knew all that? I'm not stupid Cassius, I know how things work. Every man wants to be the first one, the only one. And you ain't no different than the rest of 'em.

MUHAMMAD ALI

That's not fair Sonji. I woulda still loved you, I swear I would've.

*Enter* STEPIN FETCHIT, *with* BROTHER RASHID.

Step! There you are.

SONJI CLAY

Hey Mr. Fetchit.

STEPIN FETCHIT

Hey Sonji.

SONJI CLAY

Well, I better go.

MUHAMMAD ALI

Ok baby.

*Exit* SONJI CLAY. RASHID *closes the door and stands guard on the other side.*

MUHAMMAD ALI

Say Step, listen I wanted to ask you something. What color shorts should I wear for the workout this afternoon? Look I got two different ones right here. What ya think?

STEPIN FETCHIT

Uh well, I don't know it depends on what mood you in today.

MUHAMMAD ALI

I'm thinkin' black.

STEPIN FETCHIT

Well black it is then.

MUHAMMAD ALI

What color shorts Jack Johnson wear?

STEPIN FETCHIT

Black, always black. And sometimes pink.

MUHAMMAD ALI

Pink?

STEPIN FETCHIT

I know but he did.

MUHAMMAD ALI

Really?

STEPIN FETCHIT

Sometimes, yeah. I remember him tellin' me about his fight with Tommy Burns. Say when he came in to the ring, stripped down to just his naked black body save a pair of sizzlin' pink shorts, he say the look a' shock on Tommy's face told ole Jack that the fight was already won.

MUHAMMAD ALI

So before the first bell, a pair a' pink shorts made Jack Johnson the heavyweight champ of the world?

STEPIN FETCHIT

In a manner of speakin', yeah.

MUHAMMAD ALI

Whoa . . . Say Step, I wanted to ask you again about the Anchor Punch man. Like you sure you never heard Jack talk about somethin' like that?

STEPIN FETCHIT

I heard Jack say a lot a' things. That don't mean they were all true.

MUHAMMAD ALI

Well what did he say about, about this Anchor thing?

STEPIN FETCHIT

He said he had some kinda voodoo punch or somethin'.

MUHAMMAD ALI

Voodoo?

STEPIN FETCHIT

That's what he told me.

MUHAMMAD ALI

And you didn't believe him.

STEPIN FETCHIT

No. I mean I never saw it, and never met anybody who said they saw it so I just figured it was one of Jack's many flabbergations. You know the man lived in myth. That's just who he was as a man.

MUHAMMAD ALI

Well, I don't know if he was lyin' or not, but I tell ya I wish I had somethin' like that, you know that I could just go to, somethin' I knew would save me every time. I mean, who's to say if I can beat Liston again. I gotta stay focused, I got to 'cause if Liston sees an openin' he will exploit it.

STEPIN FETCHIT

I understand.

MUHAMMAD ALI

But really, all of this don't' mean nothin, 'cause soon the whole world is gonna end, and a little ole' bitty boxing match ain't gonna amount to a thing in the big scope of things.

STEPIN FETCHIT

You talkin' the truth now boy, see 'cause you talkin' about Judgment Day. People don't believe the word of God, but it says it right there in the Bible. And now, I don't know when it's comin', but I do hope I'm judged on everything I've done, the good and the ugly.

MUHAMMAD ALI

Me too man. And hey, I know when Judgment Day is.

STEPIN FETCHIT

Oh yeah?

MUHAMMAD ALI

Yeah it's in 1970.

STEPIN FETCHIT

What?

MUHAMMAD ALI

1970. That's when the Earth will blow up. But it ain't gonna kill all the people. Naw see 'cause ten days before the big bang, notices will be given to the righteous by way of notes in Arabic dropped from the Mothership, which will hover until 144,000 negroes are carried off into the cosmos. I gotta get to my workout. You comin'?

STEPIN FETCHIT

I wanna talk about the movie we gonna make.

MUHAMMAD ALI

I never said I was makin' a movie with you Step. (*Pause.*) I promise I'll think about it. But as far as us doin' it out there in Hollywood, see I can't see how you could wanna do that man. Like they forced you to look so stupid on that screen, made you play the lazy coon so much to where folks today cringe at the sound of your name.

STEPIN FETCHIT

Wait a minute. I was done wrong out there, but I'm proud of the Stepin Fetchit role, that's right I'm proud of Stepin Fetchit, 'cause he brought people together. Before him, white folks thought we were all savages, but through him, I proved to the White Man that he didn't have to be afraid of us.

MUHAMMAD ALI

But why should he be afraid in the first place? I mean we not lynchin' no white folks, they are killin' us. And if you proud of the way you looked up on that screen, shuffling around like a damn idiot, then maybe you are a little black Sambo.

STEPIN FETCHIT

Don't talk about me. You ain't been where I been boy don't you dare talk about me. I am the greatest actor that ever lived, 'cause I had to play my part in the shadows, had to learn to upstage the white man and out act my white partners with the most despicable, stupid lines that could come out a fellah's mouth. "Uh yes sir boss, no sir, uh?" they made me say it, but I turned shit to gold, I did that, me and my character paved the way for so much in this country, and I did it not by hatin' another man 'cause a' his prejudice, no I did it through my actin.' I snuck in the back door so you could walk in through the front, but instead what you doin? You tryina' burn the house down, you and your Nation of Islam, you . . . you know what, I'm gonna help you, 'cause I don't want the championship to go to a thug like Sonny Liston. But when you beat Sonny, and have to then go up against Floyd Patterson, I hope he knocks your ass silly.

MUHAMMAD ALI

If Floyd Patterson wants some of this, he can come on and get it!. Allah is on my side old man, so I ain't afraid of nobody!

STEPIN FETCHIT

Boy you ain't nothin' but a charlatan, you ain't no real champion.

MUHAMMAD ALI

Don't forget who you talkin' to Stepin Fetchit, or where you are . . .

STEPIN FETCHIT *stares at* ALI *who stares back. Blackout.*


*Projector screen: Fight Night*

## Scene 3

*Lights up on* STEPIN FETCHIT, *dressed in a pristine blue jacket with a pair of white pants. He admires himself in a mirror. Enter* RASHID.

BROTHER RASHID

Evening brother.

STEPIN FETCHIT

Evening.

BROTHER RASHID

Can I get you anything?

STEPIN FETCHIT

What chu mean?

BROTHER RASHID

Can I get you something to drink or eat?

STEPIN FETCHIT

Uh, no, no I'm just waiting for Ali is all.

BROTHER RASHID

Well if you need anything let me know.

STEPIN FETCHIT

Yeah alright I will.

BROTHER RASHID *turns to leave.*

STEPIN FETCHIT

Say Rashid?

BROTHER RASHID

Yes?

STEPIN FETCHIT

What you doin'?

BROTHER RASHID

Brother?

STEPIN FETCHIT

What you—boy you tryna' hustle me?

BROTHER RASHID

Hustle you? No sir. No sir not at tall. I'm just, just trying be nice. I spoke to Brother Herbert, and he say I need to be nice to you.

STEPIN FETCHIT

Why?

BROTHER RASHID

Because Brother Fetchit sir, you are my elder. And I just been remind-ed that we should not mistreat our elders, no matter who they are or what they've done. Besides brother, if I may be honest here for a sec-ond. Well, you know the old saying "let he who is without sin . . ."? Well brother I'd be the last one throwin' a stone at you. I mean, if you would've seen who I was . . . well I guess what I'm sayin is, for all the ways I've been disrespectful to you since you came up here, I wanna say I'm sorry. I apologize Mr. Fetchit.

STEPIN FETCHIT

Apology accepted Rashid.

BROTHER RASHID

And I want to extend an invitation for you to join us as a brother in the Nation of Islam.

STEPIN FETCHIT

You sure you want me, the infamous shufflin' coon, up here with yall?

BROTHER RASHID

We sure Brother Fetchit. After all, Brother Herbert reminded me that the white man is the one who made you that way. And only by follow-ing the Honorable Elijah Muhammad can we overcome the white man's visions of who we are and who we are supposed to be.

STEPIN FETCHIT

So if I join the Nation, what does that mean exactly?

BROTHER RASHID

It means you start anew. It means you let go a' your old ways, those images that people think are truly you, and instead become a full man. Also this way, we'll give you full, complete access to the champ. Anytime you want you can be with him, and anything you need, as long as we agree to it, you can have it. I heard yall talkin' about a movie, we can make that happen.

STEPIN FETCHIT

Ali ain't been too keen on the idea though.

BROTHER RASHID

Aw he'll come around, especially if your movie is approved by the Nation of Islam.

STEPIN FETCHIT

So I join the Nation and yall help me convince Ali to make this movie?

BROTHER RASHID

That is correct.

STEPIN FETCHIT

What's in it for y'all?

BROTHER RASHID

Nothin's in it for us. We want to uplift the so-called negro in this here United Snakes of America. And if upliftin' the race means helpin' an old negro actor down on his luck, why should we not then let this happen?

STEPIN FETCHIT

Sounds good to me.

BROTHER RASHID

It is good, the Nation is good. So do we have a deal?

STEPIN FETCHIT

A deal? Say Rashid, you believe the creation theory yall got, about Yacob the big head scientist?

BROTHER RASHID

Yeah, yeah I do.

STEPIN FETCHIT

And what about the one with the people who don't smile in a space-ship hoverin' up there in the sky. You believe that too?

BROTHER RASHID

Yes I do brother. I got to.

STEPIN FETCHIT

Mmmh. Rashid let me think about it.

BROTHER RASHID

Think about it? Uh ok, sounds good just uh, try to let me know before the fight alright? See this way we can announce it, tell the world that the reason you here is 'cause you have renounced the lazy shuffler that folks thought was you, to embrace the Muslim faith and become a warrior and image advisor for the Honorable Elijah Muhammad. And we want people to know the Messenger is so great, he was able to reach down and rescue from the pit of the White man's stomach the likes of you, Stepin Fetchit, the great shiftless coon turned to righteous black man by Elijah himself. See how great Elijah Muhammad is, so powerful, so omnipotent, yet merciful, he saw fit to re-imagine, re-conceptualize, and re-birth the lowly Stepin Fetchit—oh what a great night this will be. Your public conversion to Islam and Brother Ali defending his championship.

STEPIN FETCHIT

I'll think about it.

BROTHER RASHID

Sure think about it, that'll be fine.

*Enter* MUHAMMAD ALI.

STEPIN FETCHIT

Welcome Brother Fetchit. Asalamulakum Brother Muhammad sir.

MUHAMMAD ALI

Walakum-asalam Rashid.

*Exit* BROTHER RASHID.

MUHAMMAD ALI

Man he's in a good mood.

STEPIN FETCHIT

Yeah he is.

MUHAMMAD ALI

What he mean by welcome Brother Fetchit?

STEPIN FETCHIT

Oh yeah well, I've been thinkin' about uh, 'bout joinin' with the Nation of Islam.

MUHAMMAD ALI

Oh yeah, why is that?

STEPIN FETCHIT

I don't know, I just been a drifter all my life and right here with yall, this is startin' to feel like home.

MUHAMMAD ALI

Step?

STEPIN FETCHIT

Yes Brother Ali sir?

MUHAMMAD ALI

Don't do this man.

STEPIN FETCHIT

Do what Ali?

MUHAMMAD ALI

Don't be no actor right now man, stop actin'.

STEPIN FETCHIT

What I—

MUHAMMAD ALI

Man you ain't no Muslim, and you ain't never gonn' be so stop lyin' to my face.

STEPIN FETCHIT

I am gonna join the Nation. I told Rashid I'd think about it, but I am plannin' to join up.

MUHAMMAD ALI

Well then, it's a political move. 'Cause in your heart you ain't no Muslim, and you got to have it in your heart to be it. Man, I bet you got Rosary beads in your pocket, and you always talkin' about integration. That's who you are, you a integrationist, and you pray to the God of whoever integrationists pray to.

STEPIN FETCHIT

I pray to Jesus Christ.

MUHAMMAD ALI

Well there you go you pray to Jesus. You're a Christian.

STEPIN FETCHIT

But I can be Muslim, I can do it.

MUHAMMAD ALI

Step . . . Look here man, I wanna shower before the fight. If you go somewhere just meet me back here 'bout nine so we can come into the arena together.

STEPIN FETCHIT

Yeah sure, I'll just wait for you here. What time is the fight?

MUHAMMAD ALI

'Bout 10:30. I need to learn it from you.

STEPIN FETCHIT

What?

MUHAMMAD ALI

The Anchor Punch.

STEPIN FETCHIT

Boy I told you I don't know no—

MUHAMMAD ALI

9 o'clock. You gonn' teach it to me at 9 o'clock.

STEPIN FETCHIT

I can't give you what I don't have.

Exit MUHAMMAD ALI *into the shower.*

*Enter* WILLIAM FOX.

WILLIAM FOX

Hey Step, it's been a long time.

STEPIN FETCHIT

Yeah. I read what happened to you.

WILLIAM FOX

Of course, didn't everybody. The bankers, I call 'em vultures 'cause that's what they are, and they're going to run my—what do they know about movies? I know how to make 'em, you know how to act in 'em, we are the movie-makers am I right Step?

STEPIN FETCHIT

Right Mr. Fox.

WILLIAM FOX

Now could you ever imagine that they could get rid of me, but here I am back on this side.

STEPIN FETCHIT

What you want from me, sympathy?

WILLIAM FOX

No. I just would like to say to you that uh . . . well I had no problem with you. With all the prejudice this world has for the negro, instead of fighting it, you tried to turn it to your advantage, I admire a man like that. And you gave it the good fight. But I guess *we* knew, even when we were on top *we* knew the truth. We will never be greater than them. But I'm workin' on my memoirs, settin' the record straight, and looking over some different lots. Pretty soon I'll launch another studio, bigger and better than 20th Century-Fox, and what's that anyway? It's not 20th Century. I named it Fox Films after me, William Fox . . .

*Lights out on* WILLIAM FOX. *Enter* SONJI CLAY. *She approaches* RASHID *who stands stoically at the door.*

SONJI CLAY

Is Cassius in there?

BROTHER RASHID

His name is—

SONJI CLAY

Shut up Canard, I ain't got no time for your bow tie bullshit, I need to see my husband.

BROTHER RASHID

Yeah, he's in there. But don't think you can go disrespectin' me like that and call me by my slave name just 'cause you knew me when. You will treat me with respect.

SONJI CLAY

And you will get out of my way.

BROTHER RASHID

Man, I can't wait for the day when Brother Ali zips that lip and puts you in your place once and for all.

SONJI CLAY

Oh is that what you want to see Canard? Me put in my place? My husband goin' upside my head, is that what you want to see?

BROTHER RASHID

What I meant to say was—

SONJI CLAY

I know exactly what you meant. See that's why I call you Canard 'cause you ain't changed that much from your pimpin' days, nigga you still the same. All yall still just a bunch a' gangsters and you ain't foolin' nobody least of all me.

Pause.

BROTHER RASHID

Wow. Ok, that hurt Sonji. I mean, yeah I used to keep 'em in line with a backhand but that ain't me no more. No matter what you say, I have reformed. And I do my best to love my black sisters and look out for them.

SONJI CLAY

That ain't what I heard. I heard you still known to slap your wife and daughter around when you get the urge.

BROTHER RASHID

That's a lie!

SONJI CLAY

Oh it is? Hmmh, well that's not what I heard.

BROTHER RASHID

Look Sonji I ain't perfect, but I'm tryin'. I pray five times a day and I ask Allah to cleanse me of my past. But you I don't see you even tryin' to reform. You still dress and act and talk like you did when we was all in the life. And what's worse, you married to the Nation's brightest son. And I just—I don't know what Ali sees in you girl. I mean you are a fine sweet thang, yes you are, but I thought that kinda lust would've faded by now.

SONJI CLAY

It's not lust we have it's love. And you'll never understand it 'cause it's way beyond your comprehension Canard.

BROTHER RASHID

Don't push me woman.

SONJI CLAY

Or what, you gonn' strike me? You do that and my husband will kick your ass so fast, you'll be on the ground before he's finished throwin' the knockout punch.

BROTHER RASHID

Yeah ok. Same ole Sonji. But your days under his protection are numbered. Pretty soon, he's going to long for a good, decent, respectable Muslim woman, and then what you gonn' do? Ha ha back to the Silver Jack club for you. Now go take that order from the gentlemen over there, go on hustle your smile and your body for that extra tip, oh it comes so natural to you.

SONJI CLAY

I want to see my husband. Now.

> BROTHER RASHID *steps aside.* SONJI CLAY *moves past* RASHID *into the dressing room.*

SONJI CLAY

Hello Mr. Fetchit.

STEPIN FETCHIT

Hey Sonji.

SONJI CLAY

Have you seen my husband?

STEPIN FETCHIT

Yeah he's in the shower. Are you ok Sonji?

SONJI CLAY

Huh? Yeah I'm—no, no I'm not ok. I'm gonna lose him huh? I'm gonna lose my honey.

STEPIN FETCHIT

Of course not. That boy loves you girl. Every time he talks about you his eyes light up. He loves you somethin' deep. *(Pause.)* Do you feel that way about him?

SONJI CLAY

I do yeah. I wish I didn't though. 'Cause that way it would be so simple. I could just keep on bein' that thing for him in private, and the obedient wife in public. It woulda been so easy for me to play those roles, I've done it before, but with Cassius I resisted and now I know why it's 'cause I don't want us to wear no disguises, just me and him.

STEPIN FETCHIT

Well then tell 'im that.

SONJI CLAY

I think it's too late.

STEPIN FETCHIT

It ain't never too late.

*Enter* MUHAMMAD ALI *from the shower.*

SONJI CLAY

Hey baby.

MUHAMMAD ALI

Hey . . .

*They do not kiss. There is obviously tension between them.*

SONJI CLAY

Cassius, about this afternoon—

MUHAMMAD ALI

Sonji listen, I can't be with no trifflin' woman.

SONJI CLAY

Cassius—

MUHAMMAD ALI

You're an embarrassment to me. First with that outfit lookin' like a whore, and now I find out you been with every man on the south side of Chicago, just spreadin' your legs around town like some black slut. Is that what you are Sonji? A black slut?

SONJI CLAY

No I'm not a slut Cassius, I'm your wife. Mr. Fetchit, can you—

MUHAMMAD ALI

No, he ain't gotta go nowhere. Anything you wanna say to me you can now say it in front of him and all of my brothers. 'Cause we are one, me and my brothers and my sisters, we are one nation. And a nation can only rise as high as its women. And you with your lyin', wicked ways, Sonji what you doin' is holdin' us back.

SONJI CLAY

What do you mean?

MUHAMMAD ALI

You know exactly what I mean.

SONJI CLAY

Oh so, if I would've just put on the Muslim's dress and kept my mouth shut, then everything woulda been alright? Cassius baby, I'm so much more than that. There are so many parts of me that I want to share with you. And I can't go back, I can't pretend to be just a part of me no more. I gotta bring the parts of my life together baby. And I can do it, I can be smart and sexy, and a good wife, and a good mother, and I can do it under one roof. But you say we can't even buy a house 'cause in five years the Mothership's gonna come down and take people away. Well what about your honorable prophet? Elijah Muhammad has a, have you seen the size of his house? Oh so what they ain't gonn' take Elijah? Why does he get to have a house and we don't?

MUHAMMAD ALI

Sonji how many times have I told you not to ask those kinds a' questions.

SONJI CLAY

You told me you wonder if it's true your damn self.

MUHAMMAD ALI

I never said that!

SONJI CLAY

You never—? Who are you Cassius Clay? Huh? Because if you really are Muhammad Ali, then you would live what you believe, and not do one thing for them, and another when you're with me, like God can't see what you doin' . . .

   *(Pause.)*

MUHAMMAD ALI

Sonji, I'm a Muslim. And it don't feel right 'less I'm married to a woman who's in the Nation, really in the Nation. And that ain't you.

SONJI CLAY

Alright . . . so you want me to leave?

MUHAMMAD ALI

No I . . . well can you leave after the fight? 'Cause it'd be an embarrassment if you left now. Just wait till tomorrow then we'll all leave
outta here quietly. Then you can go back to Chicago and, and that's
it. Is that ok?

SONJI *ignores the question.*

SONJI CLAY

Bye Mr. Fetchit.

STEPIN FETCHIT

Bye Sonji.

SONJI *leaves the dressing room, passing* RASHID *on the
way out.*

SONJI CLAY

He's all yours.

*Exit* SONJI CLAY.

MUHAMMAD ALI

Alright Step. Whatever else you can tell me about Jack Johnson, tell
me now, 'cause me and Sonny 'bout to get it on.

STEPIN FETCHIT

Is that all you care about, learnin' all you can so you can be the
greatest?

MUHAMMAD ALI

Yeah but it's not for me, it's for my people for black people.

STEPIN FETCHIT

Bullshit! It's for you. And I ain't worthy of a mole on Jack Johnson's
elbow, but neither is you.

MUHAMMAD ALI

Why you say that Step?

STEPIN FETCHIT

Because you ain't nothin' but a selfish, whinnin' cry baby, and you'll do
anything to stay on top. You even turned your back on Malcolm X. Now

I didn't like the man myself, never could get with what he was sayin', but he was still your friend. And you turned your back on him. And now with your wife you doin' the very same thing.

MUHAMMAD ALI

That's none of your business man.

STEPIN FETCHIT

Boy look how gorgeous she is, inside and out she's pure gold. And any religion don't want you to be with a good woman like that is out of they mind.

MUHAMMAD ALI

Man you know what? I've put up with your insults and listened to your crap 'bout as much as I can. Now are you gonna tell me about Jack Johnson and what he told you, or am I gonna have to get Brother Rashid to throw you up outta here?

STEPIN FETCHIT

Nobody got to throw me out. If you do not want me here, I'm gone. Let me just go back to the motel and pack my things and I'm on the next bus to Boston.

MUHAMMAD ALI

Well I don't want you here no mo'. So please go.

STEPIN FETCHIT

Yes sir, I'm gone.

STEPIN FETCHIT *turns to leave.*

STEPIN FETCHIT

Good luck with the fight Ali.

MUHAMMAD ALI

Step, teach me the Anchor Punch man.

STEPIN FETCHIT

The Anchor—look I told you—

MUHAMMAD ALI

You done told me a lie Stepin Fetchit. Which is what you been doin' a lot of. Now you been tellin' me this and that, but I know you know the punch I'm talkin' about. And I need to learn it man. I got all kinda people on me like you wouldn't believe commin' up with ways to defeat me, so I need everything I can so I can keep on beatin' them back.

STEPIN FETCHIT

That's a losin' battle Ali. The truth is, no matter how smart you are, no matter how well trained and clever you are, you'll never have enough to defeat them. You'll end up the fool no matter what.

MUHAMMAD ALI

Muhammad Ali will never be a fool.

STEPIN FETCHIT

Maybe Muhammad Ali won't, but the Louisville Lip will, and that's what you'll be known by forever in history, the loudmouth, boastful, Louisville Lip.

MUHAMMAD ALI

That's you maybe, but that ain't me.

STEPIN FETCHIT

That's all of us! If you a negro, you're goin' down.

MUHAMMAD ALI

But I ain't no negro, I'm a black man, and I'm the heavyweight champion!

STEPIN FETCHIT

Yeah so was Jack Johnson. And he was the greatest, you ain't the greatest, he was. And still they broke him down until he was nothin', you understand? When Jack lost the belt, that young white boy hit 'im so hard, he knocked his gold teeth loose in his mouth, and Jack had to swallow his teeth to save face in front of all them white men. Now if Jack Johnson couldn't win, and I couldn't win, what the hell make you think you got any chance of being anything else but a fool?

MUHAMMAD ALI

Because I'm Muhammad Ali! I'm the greatest of them all! And you, and Johnson, and all the other champions before him is the ones that's gonna make me great. Now show me what we workin' with Step.

STEPIN FETCHIT

What about our movie?

MUHAMMAD ALI

Forget the movie. If I don't get through this weekend, a movie about my life won't even matter.

STEPIN FETCHIT

So you'll make a movie with me if you get through this weekend?

MUHAMMAD ALI

Step, man don't be like everybody else. All of 'em, Rashid, even my wife, it's like they all playin' a chess game around me. You don't think I see what everybody's been doin'? Yall think I'm that dumb? Man don't be like them man. Be my friend for real.

STEPIN FETCHIT

It ain't gonn' do no good.

MUHAMMAD ALI

Let me be the judge a' that. Man give me this and maybe this time it'll be different.

> *Pause.*

STEPIN FETCHIT

Listen.

> STEPIN FETCHIT *channels the energy of Jack Johnson.*

STEPIN FETCHIT AS JACK JOHNSON

Look at me, talkin' to my ole friend Stepin Fetchit. Fetch you better drink that drink man before I give you some of this—a deadly right, a lethal left and my secret, the Anchor Punch. Now Step, you don't wanna be on the other side of the Anchor Punch do ya?

Look here Step, I showed you all them other things right, the way I back up, retreat, hit, retreat—. My style is unorthodox yet effective. So come on Step move forward, ok and I'm backing up. But as I'm in retreat, looking like I'm about to die—"bam"—I strike back with a left jab, "bam bam" two more jabs.

Now my opponent is angry and a bit confused, 'cause when a man starts to retreat that usually signals his demise. But here I am throwin' two lefts. Now he moves at me scared, unbalanced, anxious to finish me off. And in his over zealousness, he exposes himself, drops his guard just a bit, just an inch or two but—"uh"—that's enough to get in another left and—"uh uh boo"— two more lefts and a quick right. Now he stumbles back. Stumble back Step. Stumble Step. Now, when the opponent is stunned you're supposed to go in for the kill. But I wait, see 'cause I'm not going to make any mistakes, so let's take our time with this. He moves in I strike 'im, he swings I retreat, stick stick retreat.

Alright now it's time for the kill. I go inside. What do I mean? I'm sayin'
I go deep, pass the gut to my ass and back to my lungs. I pull from all
them slaves they brought over, all the pain and beauty, and blood and
magic and faith and rage that them slaves went through see. I anchor
up to them, then I pull it through, all the way from my lungs like air to
my fist, and here it comes, riding the wind of 50 million strong—who
can dodge a punch like that? No man can withstand my Anchor Punch!

Anchor Punch.

                    STEPIN FETCHIT AND MUHAMMAD ALI
Anchor Punch
Anchor Punch
Anchor Punch
Anchor Punch
Anchor Punch
Anchor Punch
Anchor Punch
Anchor Punch

> *After many repetitions, the energy melts away as the two*
> *men stare at one another in silence.*

                         MUHAMMAD ALI
Why did it take this long? Why didn't ya show it to me when you first
got here?

                         STEPIN FETCHIT
Well I figured, once I did it for you, then you'd have no use for me. See
'cause that's all there is. As far as Jack Johnson goes you know what
I know now.

> RASHID *knocks on the door.*

                         MUHAMMAD ALI
Come in.

> *Enter* BROTHER RASHID.

                         BROTHER RASHID
Excuse me brothers. Are you all almost ready?

                         MUHAMMAD ALI
Yeah brother, we'll meet you in the hallway in one minute.

                         BROTHER RASHID
Will do Brother Ali sir.

RASHID *turns to go into the hallway.*

STEPIN FETCHI

Say Rashid, I appreciate yall offering me a place in the Nation. I really do appreciate that but, I'm a Catholic, and I always will be.

BROTHER RASHID

Do you understand what you're doing?

MUHAMMAD ALI

What he's doin' is being Stepin Fetchit, AKA Lincoln Perry- ain't that right Step?

BROTHER RASHID

But sir—

MUHAMMAD ALI

Rashid we need to stand for all black people, not just the ones that share our faith am I right?

BROTHER RASHID

I—yes, yes you are right Ali sir.

MUHAMMAD ALI

Well then Step's alright with us then. Now we'll be out there wit' ya in one second man.

BROTHER RASHID

Of course Brother Ali. Uh, we do have a few more minutes I suppose.

MUHAMMAD ALI

Thanks Rashid. Asalamalakum.

BROTHER RASHID

Walakum-asalam.

*Exit* BROTHER RASHID.

STEPIN FETCHIT

Ali, before we go out there uh, I just wanna say, I just wanna say thank you for havin' me up here as your guest. I had a good time.

MUHAMMAD ALI

You're welcome Step.

STEPIN FETCHIT

And come tomorrow mornin', I'll pack up and be on my way.

MUHAMMAD ALI

Yeah 'cause we got some interview spots to do ABC, NBC, some others too so we gotta get goin' by 7 am at the latest. Can you pack fast and be ready by 7?

STEPIN FETCHIT

Can I be ready? Boy you talkin' to the champion, king bag packer right here. So don't worry about me, I'll be ready in the lobby bright and early.

MUHAMMAD ALI

Good. And on the trip to New York, I want you and me to talk strategy for my next fight.

STEPIN FETCHIT

I'm ya man. But uh, like I said as far as.

MUHAMMAD ALI

No, I know about Jack now. No I want you with me 'cause of the knowledge you got, all the ways you've survived all this time. And I know you ain't told me all that stuff.

STEPIN FETCHIT

Oh no sir, shoot it'll take a lifetime for me to show you all the ways I been able to survive. I got techniques and methods of my own.

MUHAMMAD ALI

I know you do, so there ya go. I want you with me.

STEPIN FETCHIT

Well I most humbly accept your invitation.

MUHAMMAD ALI

Good. Alright Step, you ready?

STEPIN FETCHIT

I'm ready Champ. Oh wait, let me get a sip a' my near beer.

MUHAMMAD ALI

Alright well we gotta go.

STEPIN FETCHIT

No I know. I'll catch up with ya in the hallway.

MUHAMMAD ALI

Alright Step, see ya in a second.

> *Exit* ALI. FETCHIT *retrieves his near beer. He takes a long,*
> *satisfying sip. For a moment he stands alone, happy and*
> *completely himself. Enter* BROTHER RASHID. *He carries an*
> *old television under his arm.*

BROTHER RASHID

Goin' somwhere Mr. Fetchit?

> RASHID *sets the TV down.*

STEPIN FETCHIT

Yeah, I'm goin', I'm goin into the—

BROTHER RASHID

You don't have a seat reserved.

STEPIN FETCHIT

Why not?

BROTHER RASHID

Because it's been reassigned.

STEPIN FETCHIT

What? Aw come on man, I ain't got no time for you, man move out of
my way.

BROTHER RASHID

I shall do no such thing Stepin Fetchit.

STEPIN FETCHIT

Aw come on Rashid, I'm a be late for the fight man. Look I'm supposed
to—look Ali wants me to come in with him.

BROTHER RASHID

It's not about what Ali wants, it's about what's good for us. This whole
time you been here and you still don't get it. Now it's too late for you.

STEPIN FETCHIT

Man move—

BROTHER RASHID

No, you ain't goin' to the fight. And you and Ali? It's over. And another
thing . . .

BROTHER RASHID *grabs* STEPIN FETCHIT *brutally by his neck.*
*He squeezes* FETCHIT's *throat as he speaks in a hushed*
*whisper.*

. . . I'm tired of everybody tellin' me what to do. Herbert say I should
leave you be, I ain't lettin' you be. I don't care what Herbert or Elijah
or nobody say—no it's time for you to go Stepin Fetchit—and if you
don't, I promise, I will take your unrighteous life, I'll do it myself, is that
clear?

STEPIN FETCHIT

Yes, yes it's clear.

BROTHER RASHID *releases* STEPIN FETCHIT.

BROTHER RASHID

Now everybody wants to see the fight, after all who wouldn't? But you
will watch it here in the dressing room. Go on and watch it over there
on television.

RASHID *points to the TV he brought in.* STEPIN FETCHIT *and*
RASHID *stare at one another. Exit* BROTHER RASHID. STEPIN
FETCHIT *slowly turns away from the door. He goes to the*
*television set and turns it on. Muhammad Ali and Sonny*
*Liston are receiving the referee's instructions at the*
*center of the ring. We can hear the* TELEVISION SPORTS
ANNOUNCER *as* STEPIN FETCHIT *watches, his face illuminated*
*by the television's glow.*

TELEVISION SPORTS ANNOUNCER

. . . Our thanks to Robert Goulet, the very wonderful vocalist, and of
course Charles Sonny Liston the challenger is in the center of the
ring, and look he's staring the champion down, he's looking hard at
young Cassius! And the crowd now is booing Clay, also known as
Muhammad Ali.

Yes this is the main event folks, we're waiting for that bell for round one
(*Bell rings.*)

Here we go . . . Sonny in the dark trunks is chasing that man straight
away. Is that a mistake?

We note that early, Sonny's been shooting mostly toward that body.
You know the old story, you kill the body and the head might follow.

A knockdown ladies and gentlemen! A right hand shot, a right hand shot on the chin. Sonny can't get up.

STEPIN FETCHIT

One round!

TELEVISION SPORTS ANNOUNCER

Sonny cannot move!

STEPIN FETCHIT

One round!
One round!
One round!
One!
One!

END OF PLAY

For Overlook's complete list of plays,
or to download our drama catalog,
please visit our website:
**www.overlookny.com/drama**